Best Editorial Cartoons of the Year

KEVIN KALLAUGHER
Courtesy Baltimore Sun

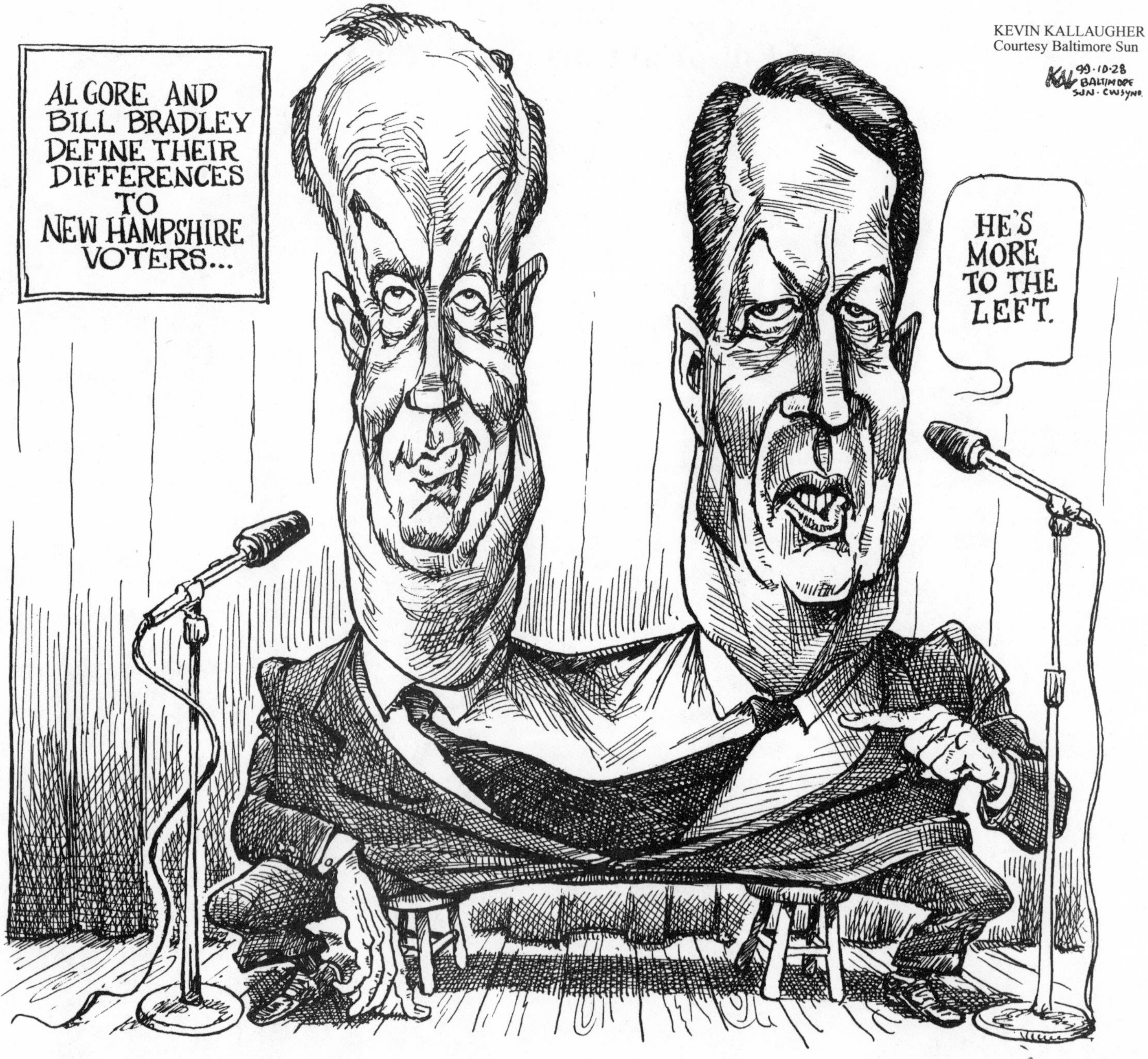
AL GORE AND BILL BRADLEY DEFINE THEIR DIFFERENCES TO NEW HAMPSHIRE VOTERS...
HE'S MORE TO THE LEFT.

BEST EDITORIAL CARTOONS OF THE YEAR

2000 EDITION

Edited by
CHARLES BROOKS

PELICAN PUBLISHING COMPANY
Gretna 2000

Library of Congress Serial Catalog Data

Best editorial cartoons. 1972-
    Gretna [La.] Pelican Pub. Co.
    v. 29 cm annual-
"A pictorial history of the year."

    1. United States—Politics and government—
1969—Caricatures and Cartoons—Periodicals.
E839.5.B45   320.9'7309240207   73-643645
ISSN 0091-2220   MARC-S

Manufactured in the United States of America
Published by Pelican Publishing Company, Inc.
1000 Burmaster Street, Gretna, Louisiana 70053

Contents

Award-Winning Cartoons

1999 PULITZER PRIZE

DAVID HORSEY

Editorial Cartoonist
Seattle Post-Intelligencer

Born in Evansville, Indiana; resident of Seattle since 1954; graduate of the University of Washington, 1976; also winner of the National Press Foundation's 1999 Berryman Award for editorial cartooning; editorial cartoonist for the *Seattle Post-Intelligencer,* 1979 to the present; syndicated in 450 newspapers by the North America Syndicate.

1999 NATIONAL HEADLINER AWARD

CLAY BENNETT

Editorial Cartoonist
The Christian Science Monitor

Born in Clinton, South Carolina, 1958; graduated from the University of North Alabama, 1980; staff artist for the *Pittsburgh Post-Gazette,* 1980-1981; editorial cartoonist and staff artist for the *Fayetteville Times* (N.C.), 1981; editorial cartoonist for the *St. Petersburg Times,* 1981-1994; editorial cartoonist for *The Christian Science Monitor,* 1997 to the present; syndicated by United Media; winner of the Mencken Award for editorial cartooning, 1986.

1998 NATIONAL SOCIETY OF PROFESSIONAL JOURNALISTS AWARD

(Selected in 1999)

JACK HIGGINS

Editorial Cartoonist
Chicago Sun-Times

Graduate of the College of Holy Cross, 1976; editorial cartoonist for the
Chicago Sun-Times, 1984 to the present; winner of Sigma Delta Chi
National Society of Professional Journalists Award, 1988; Pulitzer Prize,
1989; and Fischetti Award for editorial cartoons, 1998.

1999 FISCHETTI AWARD

NICK ANDERSON

Editorial Cartoonist
Louisville Courier-Journal

Native of Toledo, Ohio; studied political science at Ohio State University and drew cartoons for the university newspaper; won Charles M. Schulz Award as the best college cartoonist, 1989; editorial cartoonist for the *Louisville Courier-Journal,* 1990 to the present.

1998 NATIONAL NEWSPAPER AWARD / CANADA
(Selected in 1999)

ROY PETERSON

Editorial Cartoonist
Vancouver Sun

Born in Winnipeg, 1936; editorial cartoonist for the *Vancouver Sun,* 1962 to the present; previous six-time winner of Canada's National Newspaper Award, in 1968, 1975, 1984, 1990, 1994, and 1996; winner of the International Salon of Cartoons Grand Prize, 1973; book illustrator; author of three books; president of the Association of American Editorial Cartoonists, 1982-1983.

Best Editorial Cartoons of the Year

Berry's World

© 1999 by NEA, Inc.

"Good news! Our poll shows that, if you are removed from office, your Approval Rating will hit 85 percent."

The Clinton Administration

After a full year of investigations, hearings, and a 21-day impeachment trial, President Clinton was acquitted by the U.S. Senate of charges he had committed perjury and obstructed justice. Judge Susan Webber Wright, however, found Clinton in contempt of court for giving "false, misleading, and evasive answers that were designed to obstruct the judicial process." She ordered the president to pay $90,686 for giving false testimony in a harassment lawsuit filed by Paula Jones. Shortly after the Senate acquittal, a woman named Juanita Broaddrick claimed Clinton had raped her in 1978, but nothing came of the charge.

The Clinton Administration filed a civil action against Big Tobacco for billions, and the FBI belatedly admitted having fired incendiary devices at Waco—something that had long been denied.

Pope John Paul II visited St. Louis, Missouri, where he met with Clinton. The irony of the meeting between the famous saint and the infamous sinner could not be overlooked.

President Clinton offered clemency to several jailed Puerto Rican terrorists convicted of sedition. His wife, Hillary, who was considering a run for the U.S. Senate in New York, applauded the move then later criticized it. The president also vetoed the Republican tax cut bill, and was humiliated when Congress rejected the Comprehensive Test Ban Treaty.

GARY BROOKINS
Courtesy Richmond Times-Dispatch

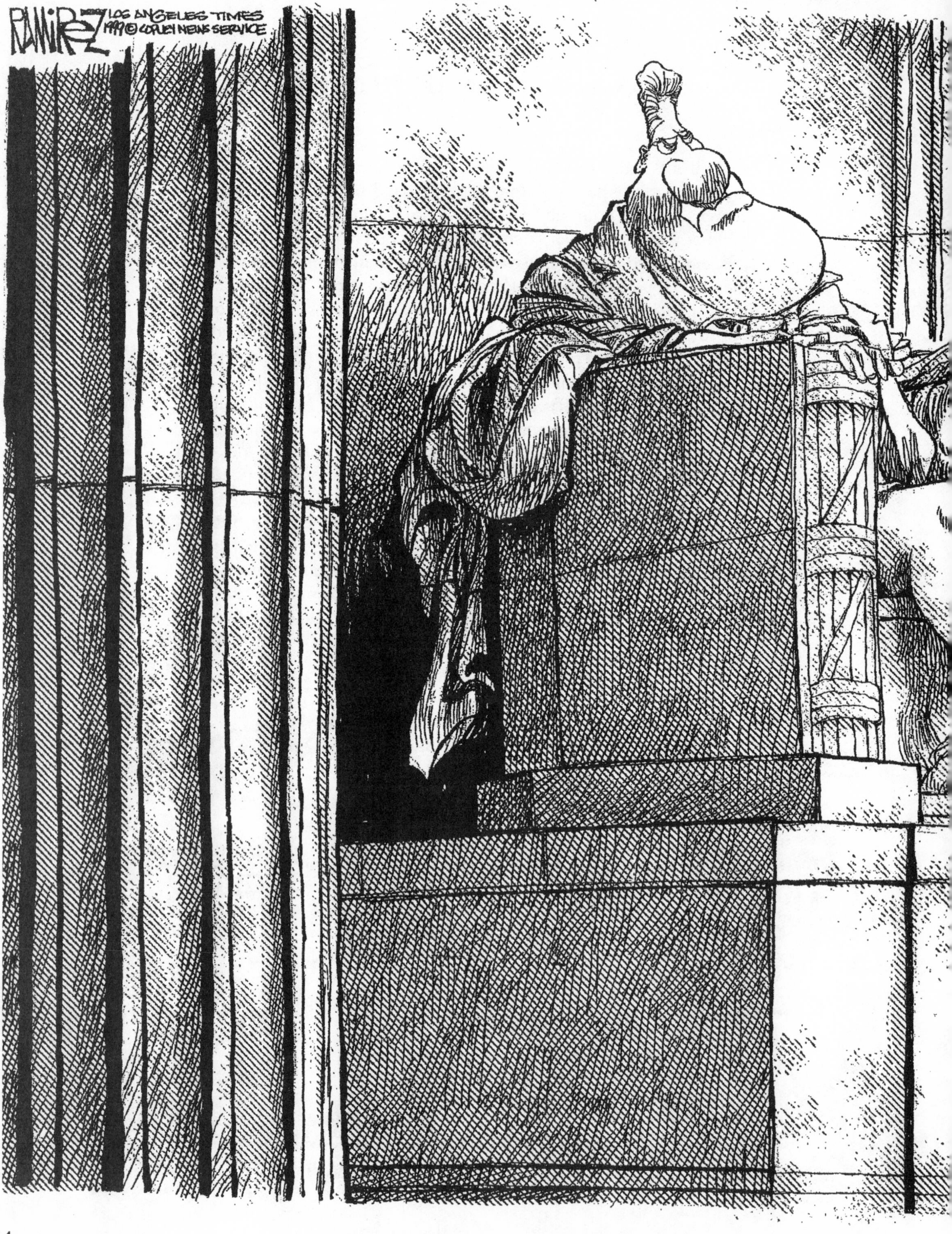
RAMIREZ
LOS ANGELES TIMES
1999 © COPLEY NEWS SERVICE

CONTEMPT

MICHAEL RAMIREZ
Courtesy Los Angeles Times

BRIAN DUFFY
Courtesy Des Moines Register

VIC HARVILLE
Courtesy Arkansas Democrat-Gazette

GARY BROOKINS
Courtesy Richmond Times-Dispatch

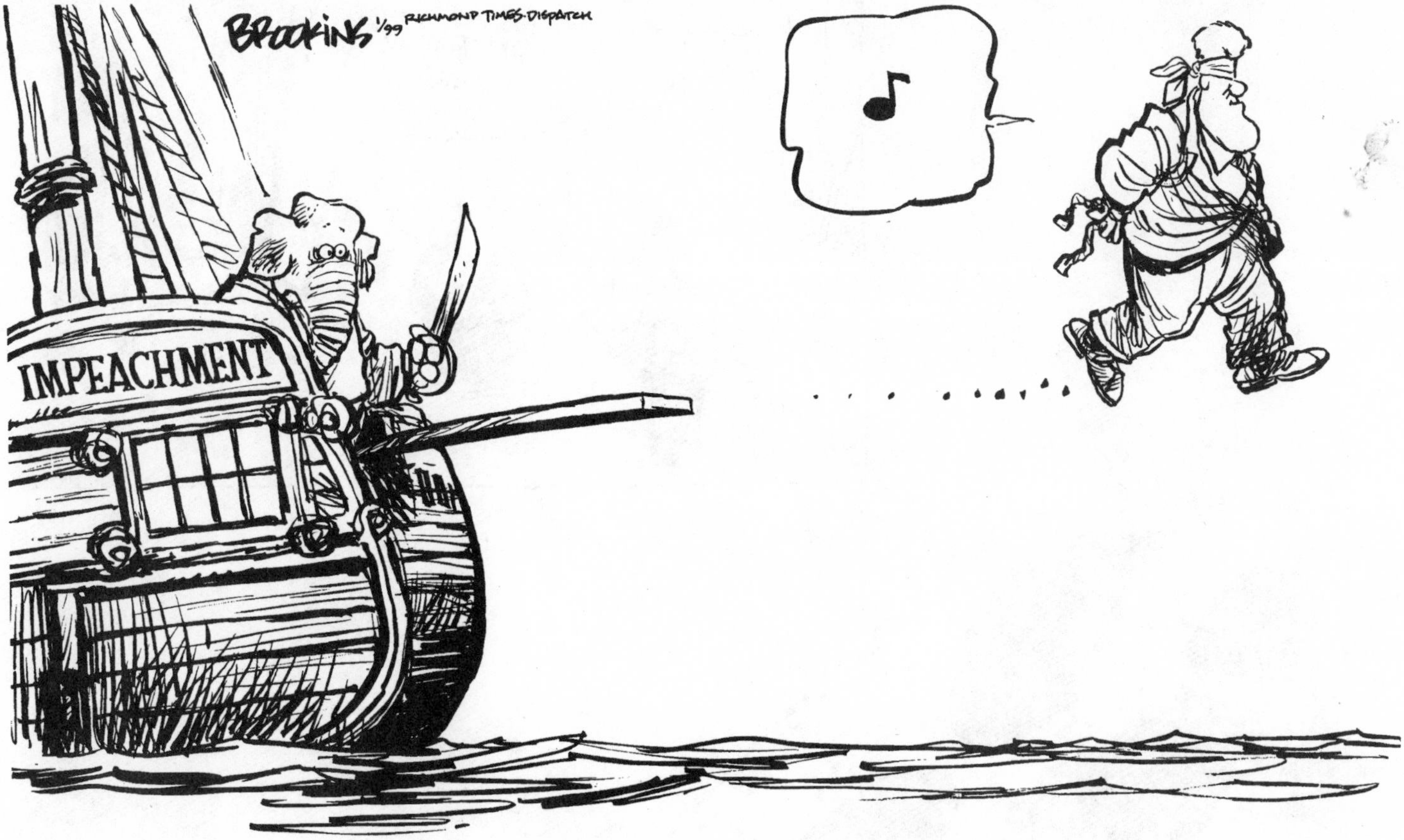

BROOKINS 1/99 RICHMOND TIMES-DISPATCH
♪
IMPEACHMENT

STEVE KELLEY
Courtesy San Diego Union

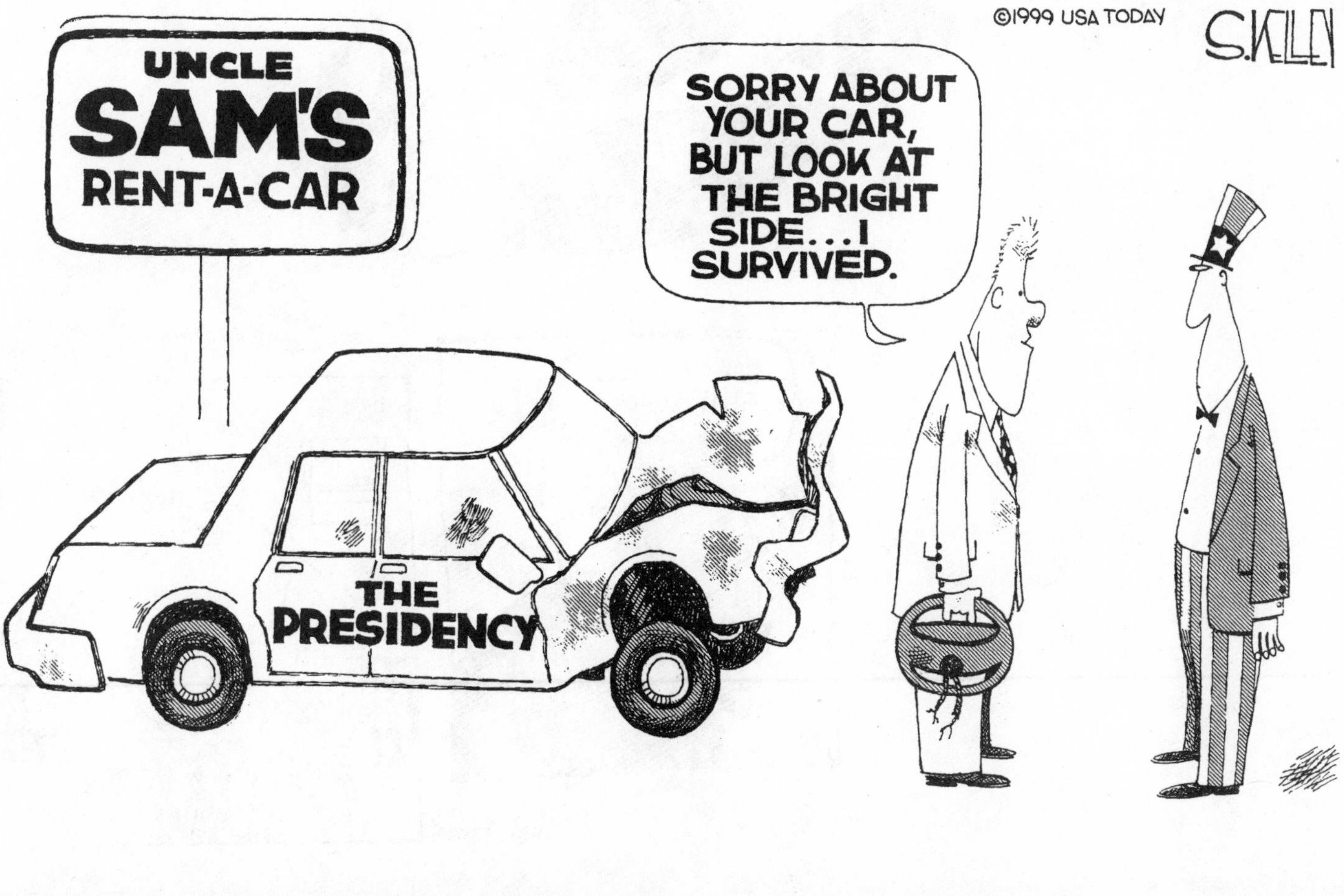

©1999 USA TODAY
S.KELLEY
UNCLE SAM'S RENT-A-CAR
SORRY ABOUT YOUR CAR, BUT LOOK AT THE BRIGHT SIDE...I SURVIVED.
THE PRESIDENCY

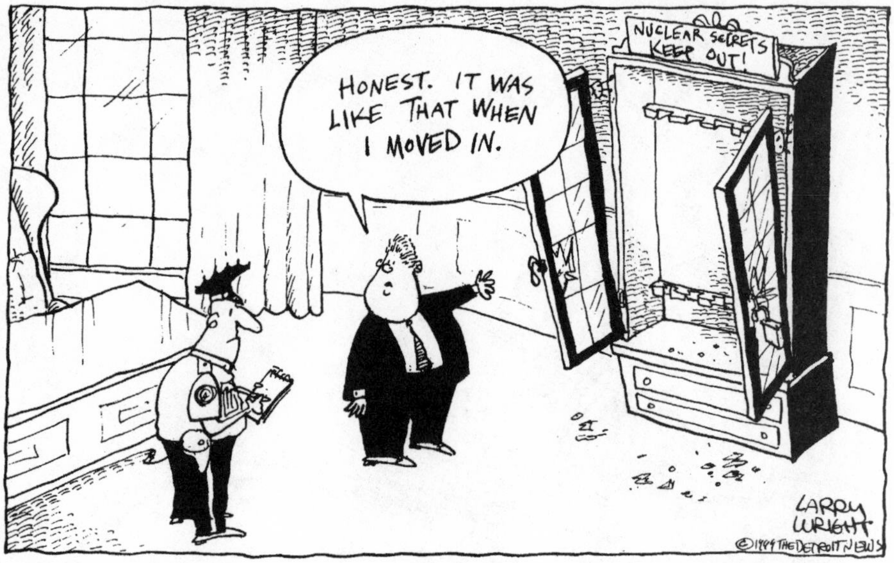
NUCLEAR SECRETS KEEP OUT!
HONEST. IT WAS LIKE THAT WHEN I MOVED IN.
LARRY WRIGHT
©1999 THE DETROIT NEWS

LARRY WRIGHT
Courtesy Detroit News

JIM BORGMAN
Courtesy Cincinnati Enquirer

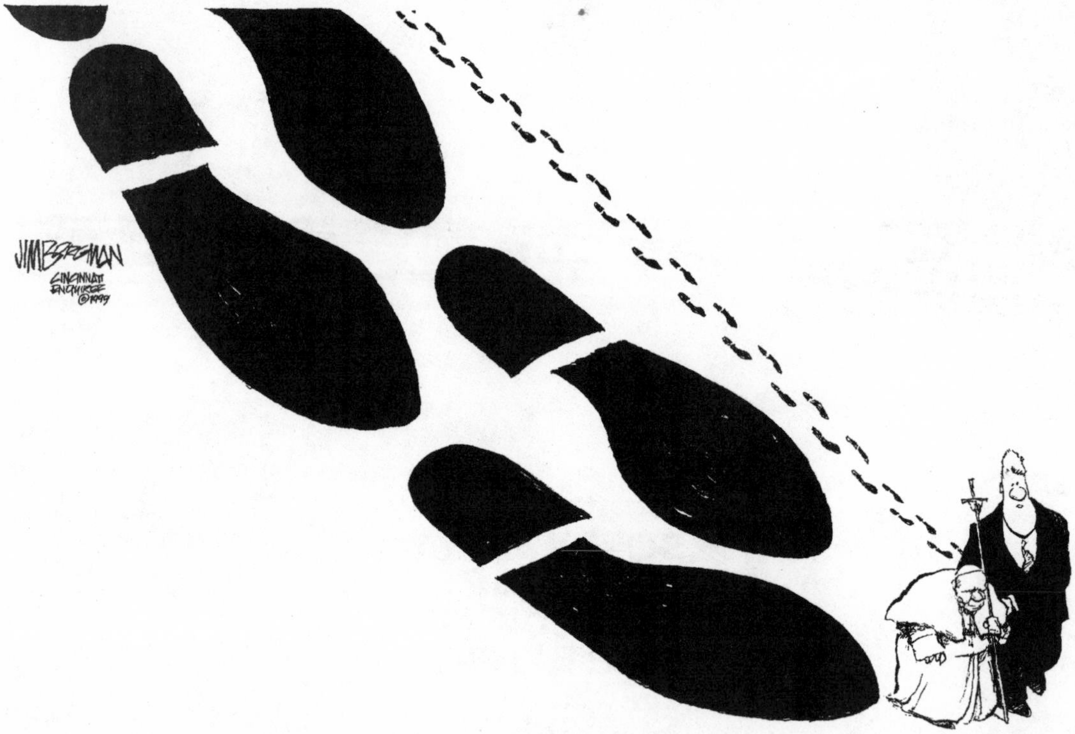
JIM BORGMAN
CINCINNATI ENQUIRER
©1999

SIGNE WILKINSON
Courtesy Philadelphia Daily News

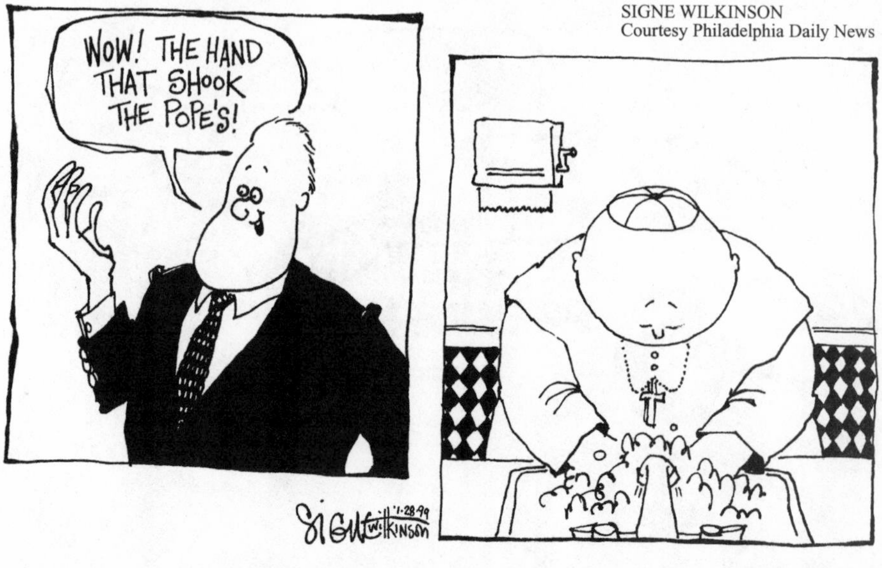
WOW! THE HAND THAT SHOOK THE POPE'S!
SIGNE WILKINSON 1·28·99

KEN DAVIS
Courtesy Cedartown Standard (Ga.)

SCOTT STANTIS
Courtesy Birmingham News

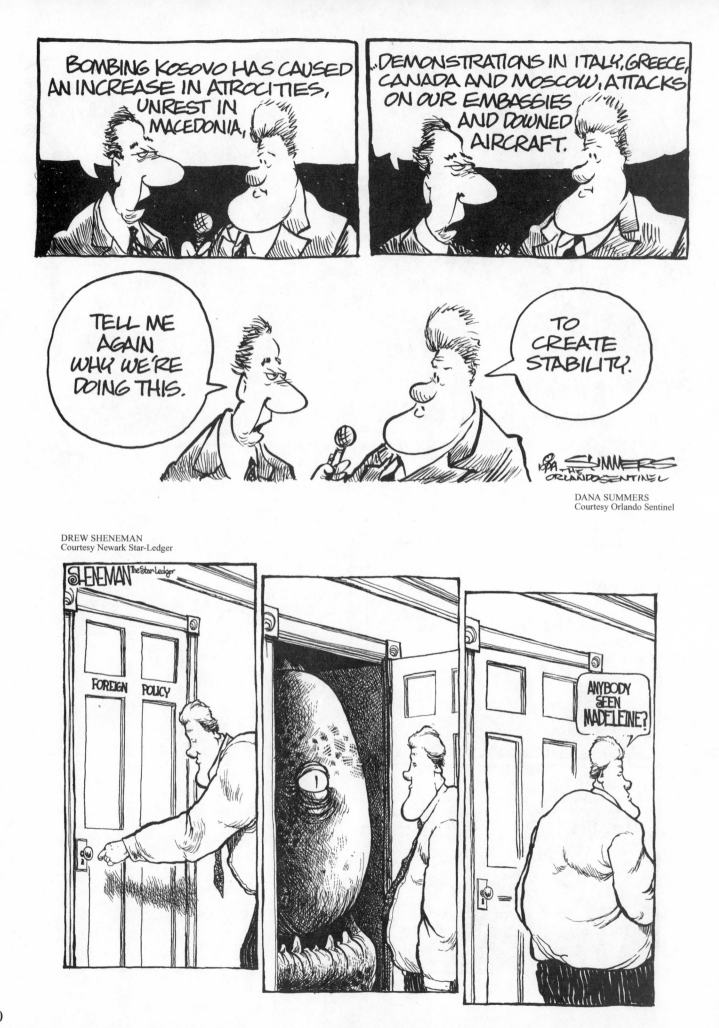

DANA SUMMERS
Courtesy Orlando Sentinel

DREW SHENEMAN
Courtesy Newark Star-Ledger

ROGER SCHILLERSTROM
Courtesy Crain Communications

GARY VARVEL
Courtesy Indianapolis Star

BOB GORRELL
Courtesy Creators Syndicate
©1999 CREATORS SYNDICATE INC.
WWW.CREATORS.COM

EDGAR SOLLER
Courtesy California Examiner

VIC CANTONE
Courtesy Brooklyn Papers Publications

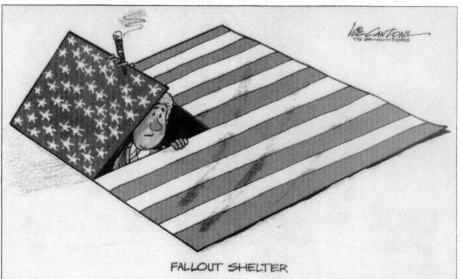

GOD CERTAINLY DIDN'T HELP PRESIDENT CLINTON DEFEAT THIS GIANT
... SO, HE MUST BE GETTING HIS HELP FROM THE OTHER FELLOW.

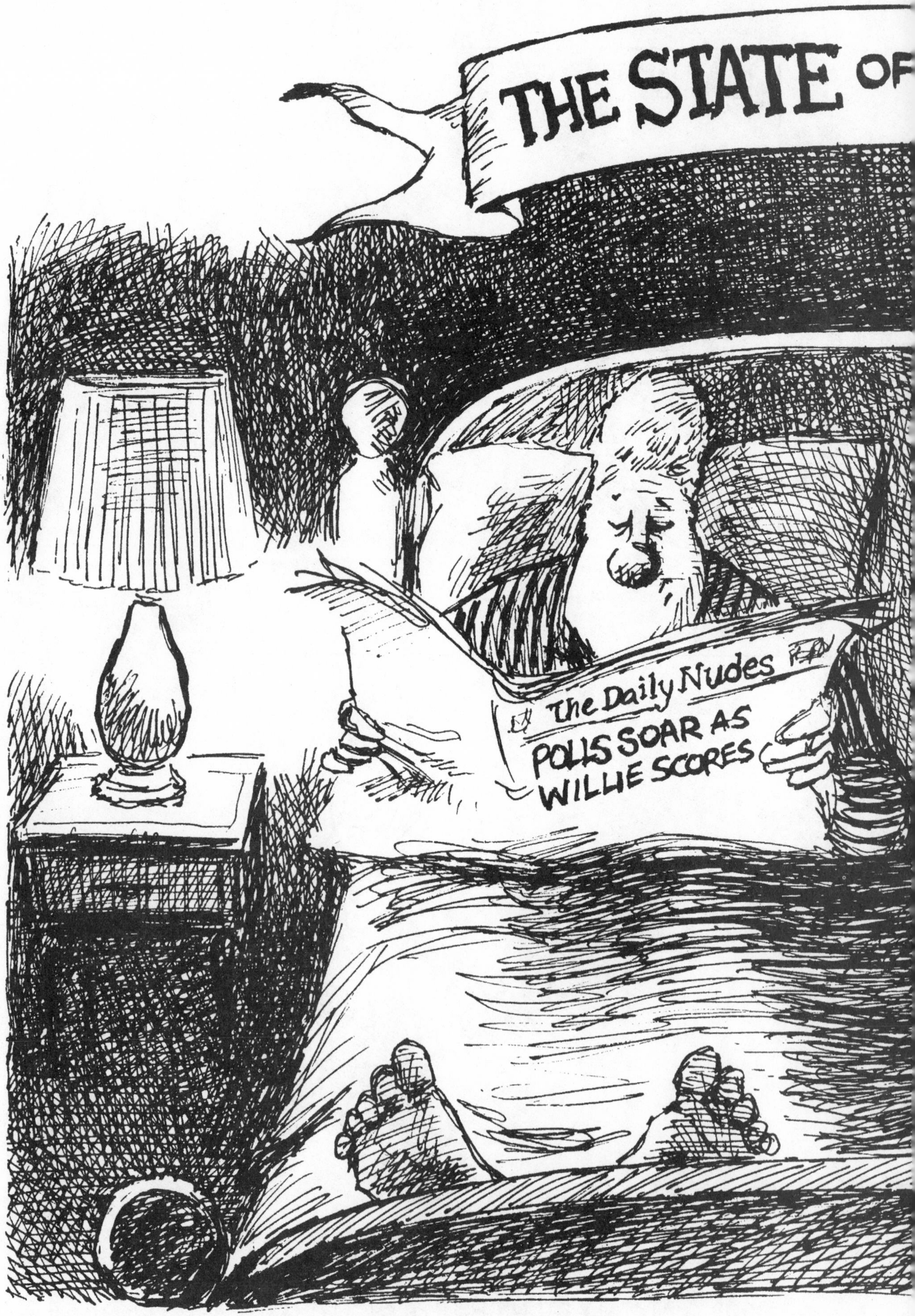
THE STATE OF
The Daily Nudes
POLLS SOAR AS WILLIE SCORES

JACK HIGGINS
Courtesy Chicago Sun-Times

STEVE GREENBERG
Courtesy Seattle Post-Intelligencer

JOE MAJESKI
Courtesy Wilkes-Barre Times Leader

26

DAVID HORSEY
Courtesy Seattle Post-Intelligencer

FRANK CAMMUSO
Courtesy Syracuse Herald-Journal

27

JACK JURDEN
Courtesy Wilmington News Journal

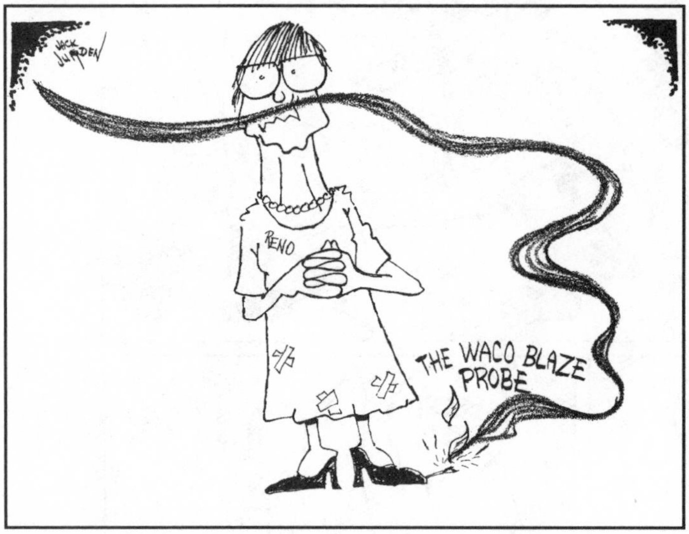
RENO
THE WACO BLAZE PROBE

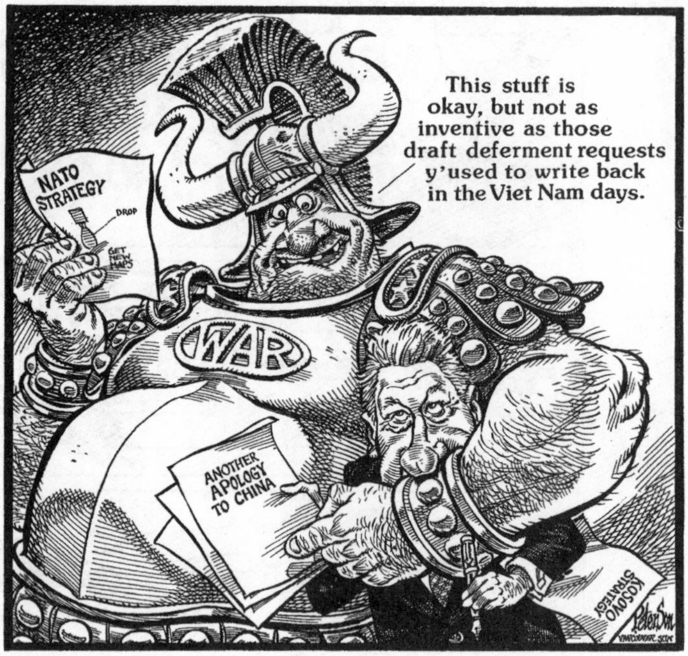
This stuff is okay, but not as inventive as those draft deferment requests y'used to write back in the Viet Nam days.
NATO STRATEGY
DROP
WAR
ANOTHER APOLOGY TO CHINA
KOSOVO STRATEGY

ROY PETERSON
Courtesy Vancouver Sun

KEVIN KALLAUGHER
Courtesy Baltimore Sun

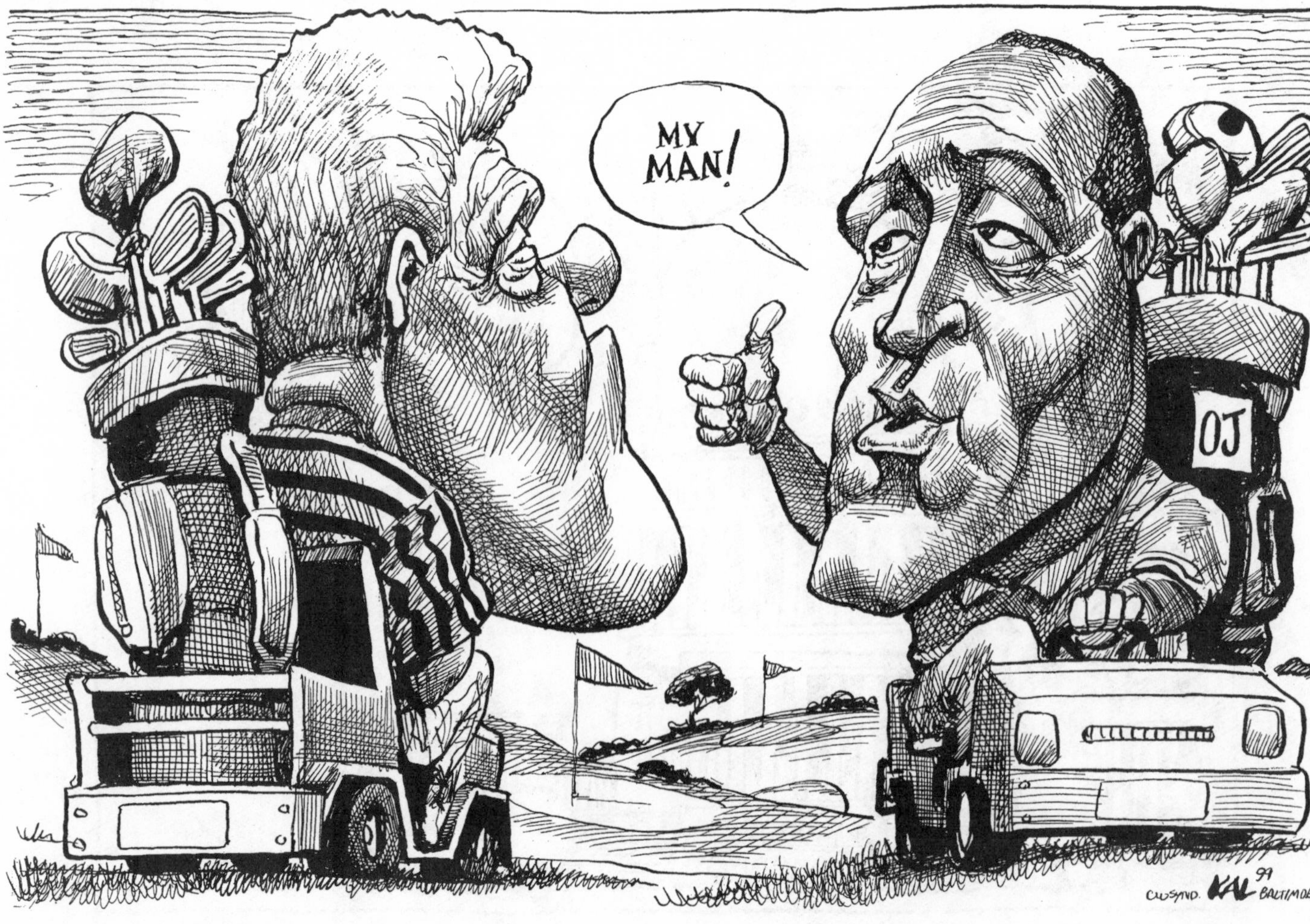
MY MAN!
OJ

JEFF MacNELLY
Courtesy Chicago Tribune

MACNELLY Chicago Tribune macnelly.com
War on Drugs II
TOBACCO
DOJ

SCOTT STANTIS
Courtesy Birmingham News

©1999 THE BIRMINGHAM NEWS COPLEY NEWS SERVICE STANTIS
COME BACK WHEN YOU'VE BEEN RAPED BY A REPUBLICAN!
BROADDRICK
NOW
FEMINISTS

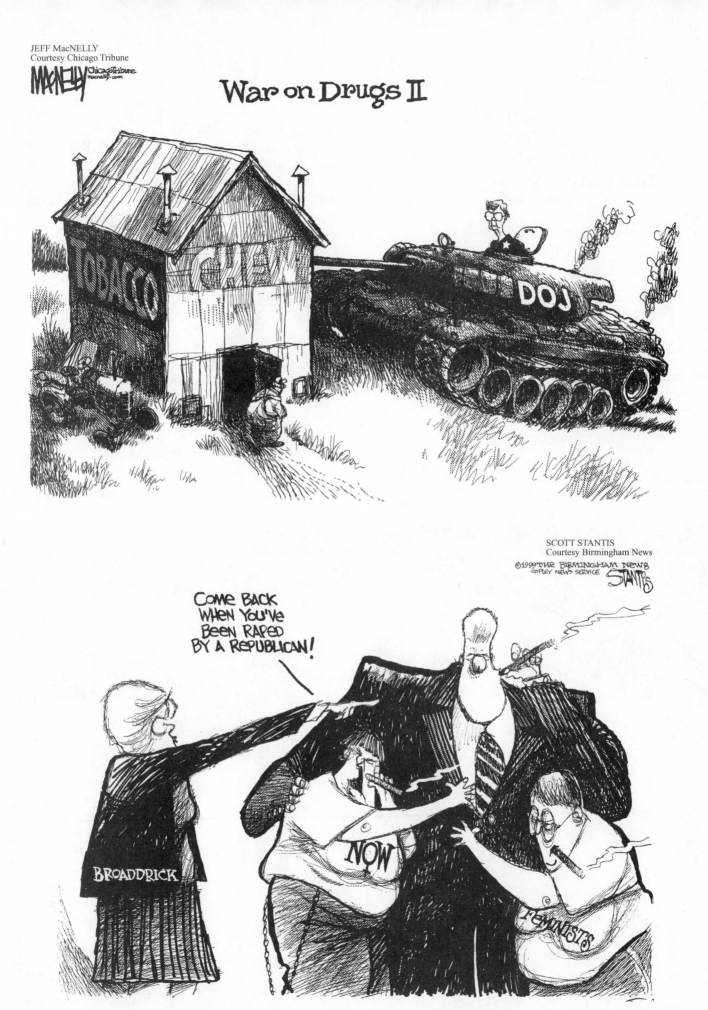

JIM BERRY
Courtesy NEA

CHIP BECK
Courtesy Political Graphics & News Service

NICK ANDERSON
Courtesy Louisville Courier-Journal

MIKE PETERS
Courtesy Dayton Daily News

MARK THORNHILL
Courtesy North County Times (Calif.)

THE "EMPEROR'S" NEW CLOTHES

JIM LANGE
Courtesy Daily Oklahoman

RICK KOLLINGER
Courtesy Easton Star Democrat

SCOTT NICKEL
Courtesy Antelope Valley Press

GARY VARVEL
Courtesy Indianapolis Star

JEFF MacNELLY
Courtesy Chicago Tribune

33

BILL GARNER
Courtesy Washington Times

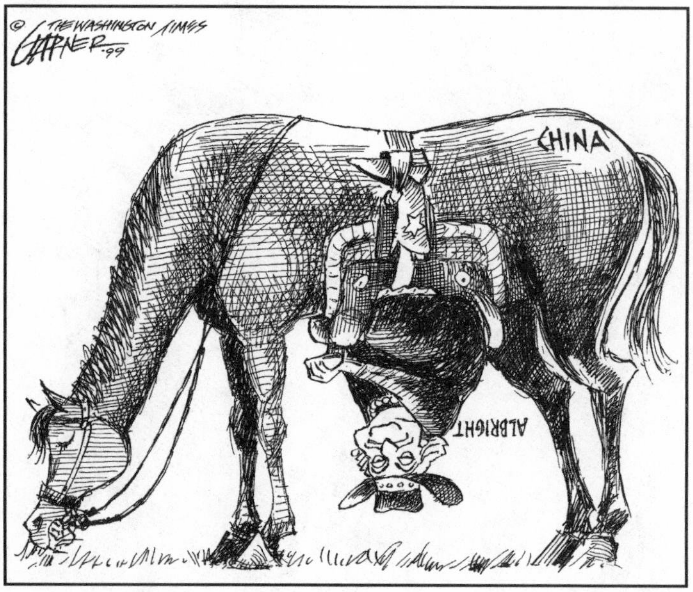
© THE WASHINGTON TIMES
GARNER '99
CHINA
ALBRIGHT

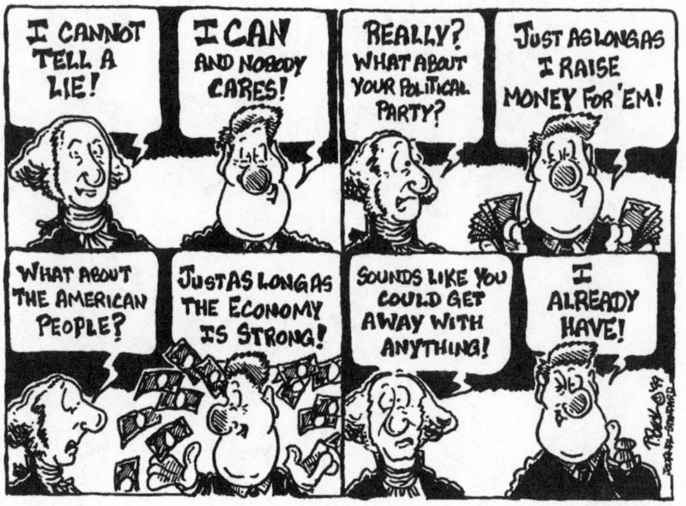
I CANNOT TELL A LIE!
I CAN AND NOBODY CARES!
REALLY? WHAT ABOUT YOUR POLITICAL PARTY?
JUST AS LONG AS I RAISE MONEY FOR 'EM!
WHAT ABOUT THE AMERICAN PEOPLE?
JUST AS LONG AS THE ECONOMY IS STRONG!
SOUNDS LIKE YOU COULD GET AWAY WITH ANYTHING!
I ALREADY HAVE!

TOM BECK
Courtesy Freeport Journal-Standard (Ill.)

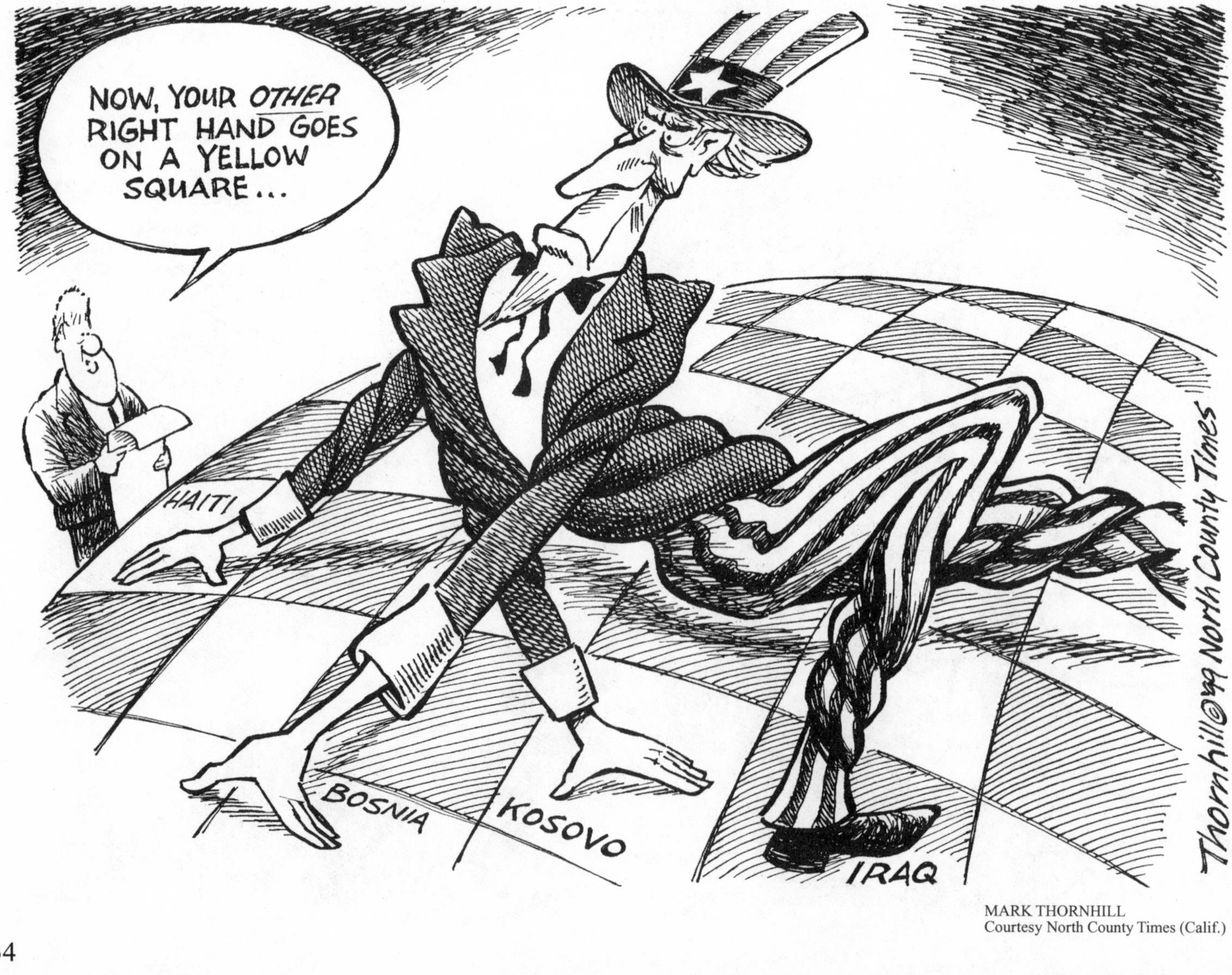
NOW, YOUR OTHER RIGHT HAND GOES ON A YELLOW SQUARE...
HAITI
BOSNIA
KOSOVO
IRAQ
Thornhill ©99 North County Times

MARK THORNHILL
Courtesy North County Times (Calif.)

BROOKINS RICHMOND TIMES-DISPATCH 9/99

Tarnished Badge

ED GAMBLE
Courtesy Florida Times-Union

HITCH YOUR WAGON TO A STARR...

Politics

The 2000 presidential campaign got underway in earnest with a broad field of Republican challengers that included George W. Bush, John McCain, Elizabeth Dole, Steve Forbes, Dan Quayle, Pat Buchanan, and Lamar Alexander. At year's end, however, only Bush, McCain, and Forbes remained standing. Hillary Clinton announced she would run for the U.S. Senate from New York, and the Clintons purchased a $2.2 million home there to establish residence.

Actor Warren Beatty and financier Donald Trump threatened to become presidential candidates, but at the end of the year seemed to have faded from the scene. Vice President Gore, lagging early in the polls, packed up his Washington campaign headquarters and moved it to Nashville, Tennessee. The Bush campaign tried to distance itself from congressional Republicans because of what the candidate perceived as their sellout to Clinton on many issues. Pat Buchanan bolted to the Reform Party for similar reasons.

Jesse Ventura, the controversial Reform Party governor of Minnesota, angered many people by his remarks in a *Playboy* magazine interview. The former professional wrestler declared that organized religion was "for weak-minded people." He also defended the perpetrators of the infamous Tailhook scandal.

NICK ANDERSON
Courtesy Louisville Courier-Journal

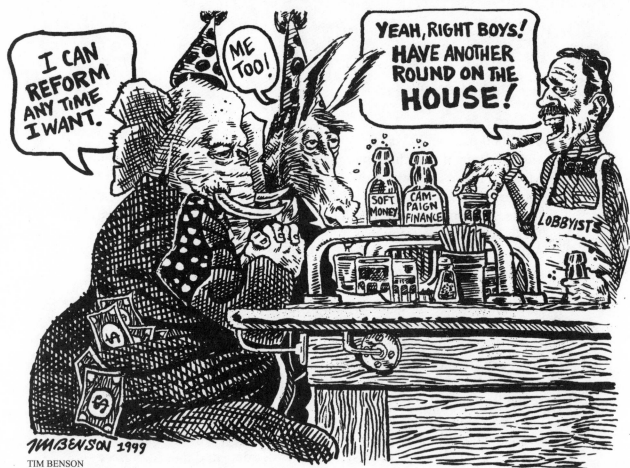

TIM BENSON
Courtesy Argus Leader (S.D.)

MIKE KEEFE
Courtesy Denver Post

EUGENE PAYNE
Courtesy Charlotte Observer

ROBERT ARIAIL
Courtesy The State (S.C.)

RICHARD CROWSON
Courtesy Wichita Eagle

JERRY BARNETT
Courtesy Indianapolis News

STEVE BREEN
Courtesy Asbury Park Press (N.J.)

REX BABIN
Courtesy Sacramento Bee

LINDA BOILEAU
Courtesy Frankfort State Journal

J. R. ROSE
Courtesy Byrd Newspapers

JIM DYKE
Courtesy News Tribune (Mo.)

JOE HELLER
Courtesy Green Bay Press-Gazette

MIKE KEEFE
Courtesy Denver Post

BOB GORRELL
Courtesy Creators Syndicate

JERRY BUCKLEY
Courtesy Express Newspapers

BOB RICH
Courtesy Connecticut Post

TED RALL
Courtesy San Francisco Examiner

DICK LOCHER
Courtesy Chicago Tribune

MARK THORNHILL
Courtesy North County Times (Calif.)

JIM BERRY
Courtesy NEA

IF TODAY'S POLITICIANS HAD BEEN AROUND IN 1776

CHUCK ASAY
Courtesy Colorado Springs Gazette-Telegraph

JOHN SHERFFIUS
Courtesy St. Louis Post-Dispatch

BOB GORRELL
Courtesy Creators Syndicate
©1999 CREATORS SYNDICATE INC.
WWW.CREATORS.COM
GORRELL

CHARLIE DANIEL
Courtesy Knoxville News-Sentinel

MILT PRIGGEE
Courtesy Spokane Spokesman-Review

BILL MANGOLD
Courtesy Saline Reporter (Mich.)

DANA SUMMERS
Courtesy Orlando Sentinel

49

JOE LONG
Courtesy Observer-Dispatch (N.Y.)

JIM LANGE
Courtesy Daily Oklahoman

SCOTT BATEMAN
Courtesy North American Syndicate

JOE MAJESKI
Courtesy Wilkes-Barre Times Leader

JACK OHMAN
Courtesy The Oregonian

51

SAM RAWLS
Courtesy Rockdale Citizen (Ga.)

JOHN BRANCH
Courtesy San Antonio Express-News

WILLIAM L. FLINT
Courtesy Arlington Morning News

POST-IMPEACHMENT FALLOUT

DOUG MacGREGOR
Courtesy News-Press at Fort Myers

MICKEY SIPORIN
Courtesy Newark Star-Ledger

JESSE (THE POLITICIAN) VENTURA

PARTY SYMBOLS

THE DES MOINES REGISTER

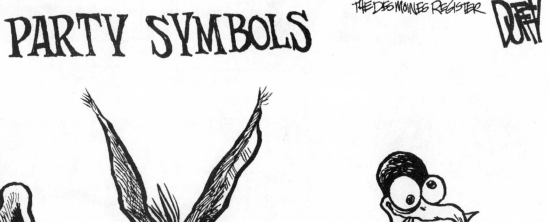

REPUBLICAN ELEPHANT

DEMOCRATIC DONKEY

REFORM LOON

BRUCE BEATTIE
Courtesy Daytona Beach News-Journal

©99 Daytona Beach News-Journal
Copley News Service
N-JCENTER.COM BEATTIE

"I'm a compassionate conservative . . . so in addition to 'GET LOST,'
I'd like to add, 'HAVE A NICE DAY.' "

HAVING STUMPED GEORGE W. WITH A FOREIGN POLICY POP QUIZ, THE MEDIA TRIES TO DO THE SAME WITH A DOMESTIC TEST!

ED GAMBLE
Courtesy Florida Times-Union

BEN SARGENT
Courtesy Austin American-Statesman

ETTA HULME
Courtesy Fort Worth Star-Telegram

STEVE KELLEY
Courtesy San Diego Union

56

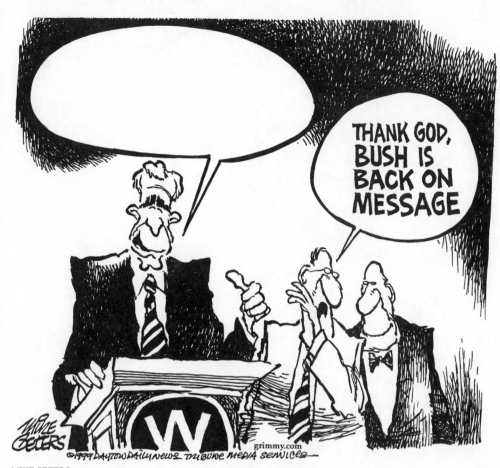

MIKE PETERS
Courtesy Dayton Daily News

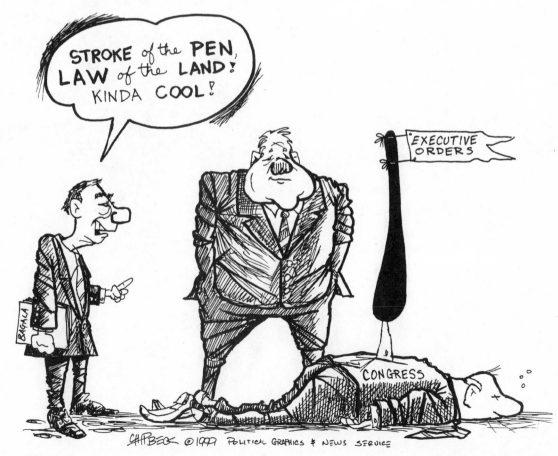

CHIP BECK
Courtesy Political Graphics & News Service

HANK McCLURE
Courtesy Lawton Constitution (Okla.)

GLENN McCOY
Courtesy Belleville News-Democrat

The Democrats

Al Gore's campaign for the Democratic nomination for president got off to a slow start. His speeches were seen by voters and the media as stiff and dull. He referred to Bill Clinton as one of America's greatest presidents. But when that did not resonate with voters, he began to put distance between him and his boss. In an effort to boost his campaign, he moved his headquarters to Tennessee and began dressing more casually and speaking in a more folksy manner.

For Gore, however, the Clinton stain seemed hard to erase, and opponent Bill Bradley's campaign picked up steam. Following debates between Gore and Bradley at Dartmouth College, polls gave Dollar Bill a narrow edge over the vice president among likely Democratic primary voters in New Hampshire.

Public Broadcasting Service was caught sharing its donor lists with political groups. It was disclosed that 30 of the nation's 349 PBS stations had secretly provided lists of donors to branches of the Democratic Party and to various groups supporting Democratic causes.

Republican members of Congress threatened to withhold funding from PBS because of the controversy. Experts agreed that it could be a violation of the tax laws if both political parties did not receive equal access to the lists.

STEVE BREEN
Courtesy Asbury Park Press (N.J.)

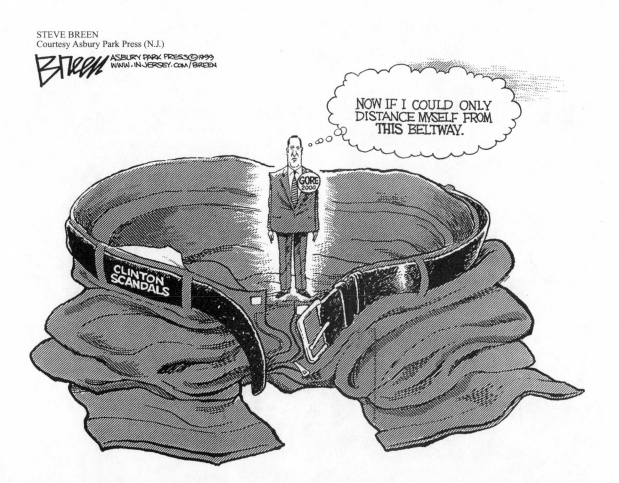

59

WAYNE STAYSKAL
Courtesy Tampa Tribune

CLAY JONES
Courtesy Free Lance-Star (Va.)

60

WALT HANDELSMAN
Courtesy New Orleans Times-Picayune

...IN AN EFFORT TO GARNER HEADLINES OF HIS OWN, AL GORE TRIES SNORTING COKE...

JACK OHMAN
Courtesy The Oregonian

THE HARDSCRABBLE YEARS OF AL GORE...

"When I was seven, I often had to cash a T-Bill to go to the movies..."

"My father worked in a loud sweatshop..."

...POINT OF ORDER, SENATOR!

HOW MUCH MORE CAN I ENDURE?

"I would often do field work while I was in college..."

"I worked menial jobs..."

HARVARD

...GO LONG, AL!!!

Z.

VICE PRESIDE

JERRY BARNETT
Courtesy Indianapolis News

VIC HARVILLE
Courtesy Arkansas Democrat-Gazette

NICK ANDERSON
Courtesy Louisville Courier-Journal

DICK LOCHER
Courtesy Chicago Tribune

MICHAEL RAMIREZ
Courtesy Los Angeles Times

63

DAVID HITCH
Courtesy Worcester Telegram & Gazette (Mass.)

JEFF PARKER
Courtesy Florida Today

DAVID HORSEY
Courtesy Seattle Post-Intelligencer

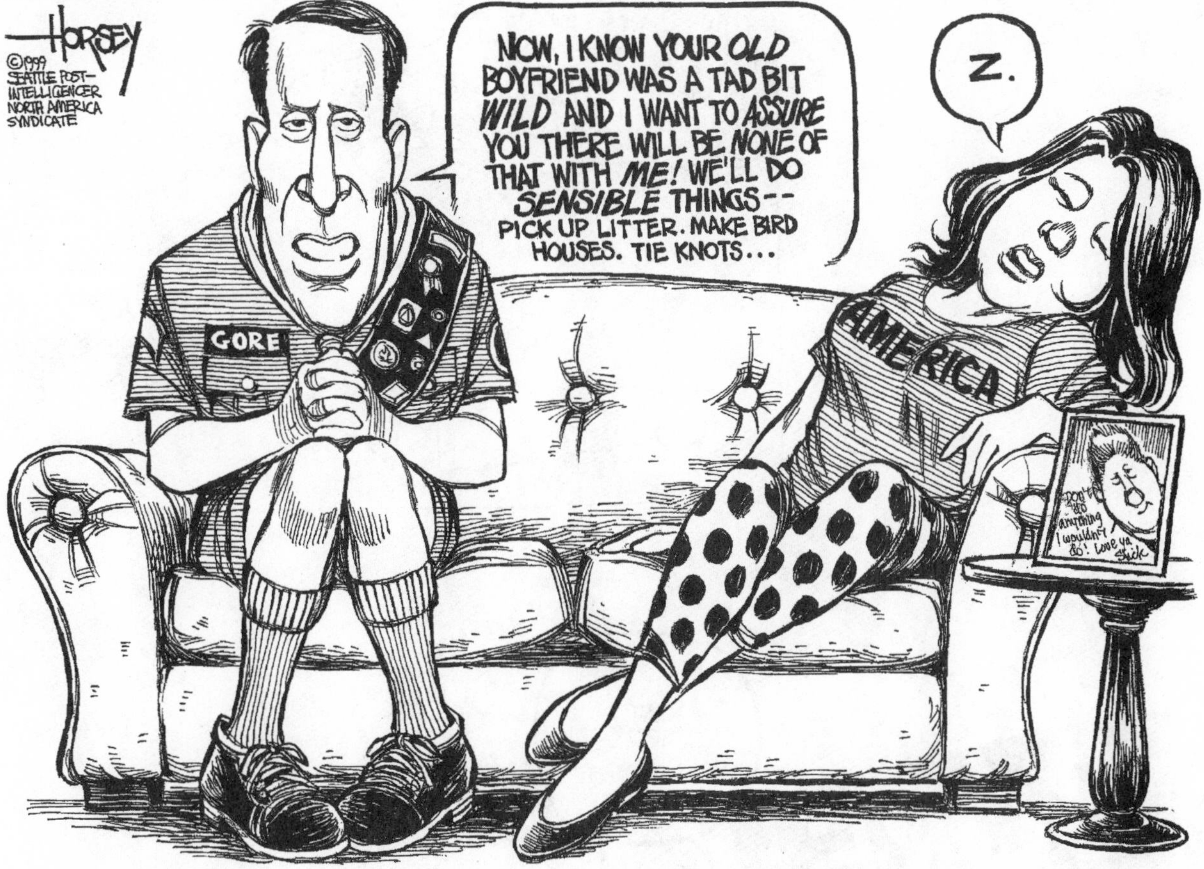
HORSEY
©1999 SEATTLE POST-INTELLIGENCER NORTH AMERICA SYNDICATE
NOW, I KNOW YOUR OLD BOYFRIEND WAS A TAD BIT WILD AND I WANT TO ASSURE YOU THERE WILL BE NONE OF THAT WITH ME! WE'LL DO SENSIBLE THINGS-- PICK UP LITTER. MAKE BIRD HOUSES. TIE KNOTS...
Z.
GORE
AMERICA
Don't do anything I wouldn't do! Love ya Slick

JAMES CASCIARI
Courtesy Vero Beach Press Journal

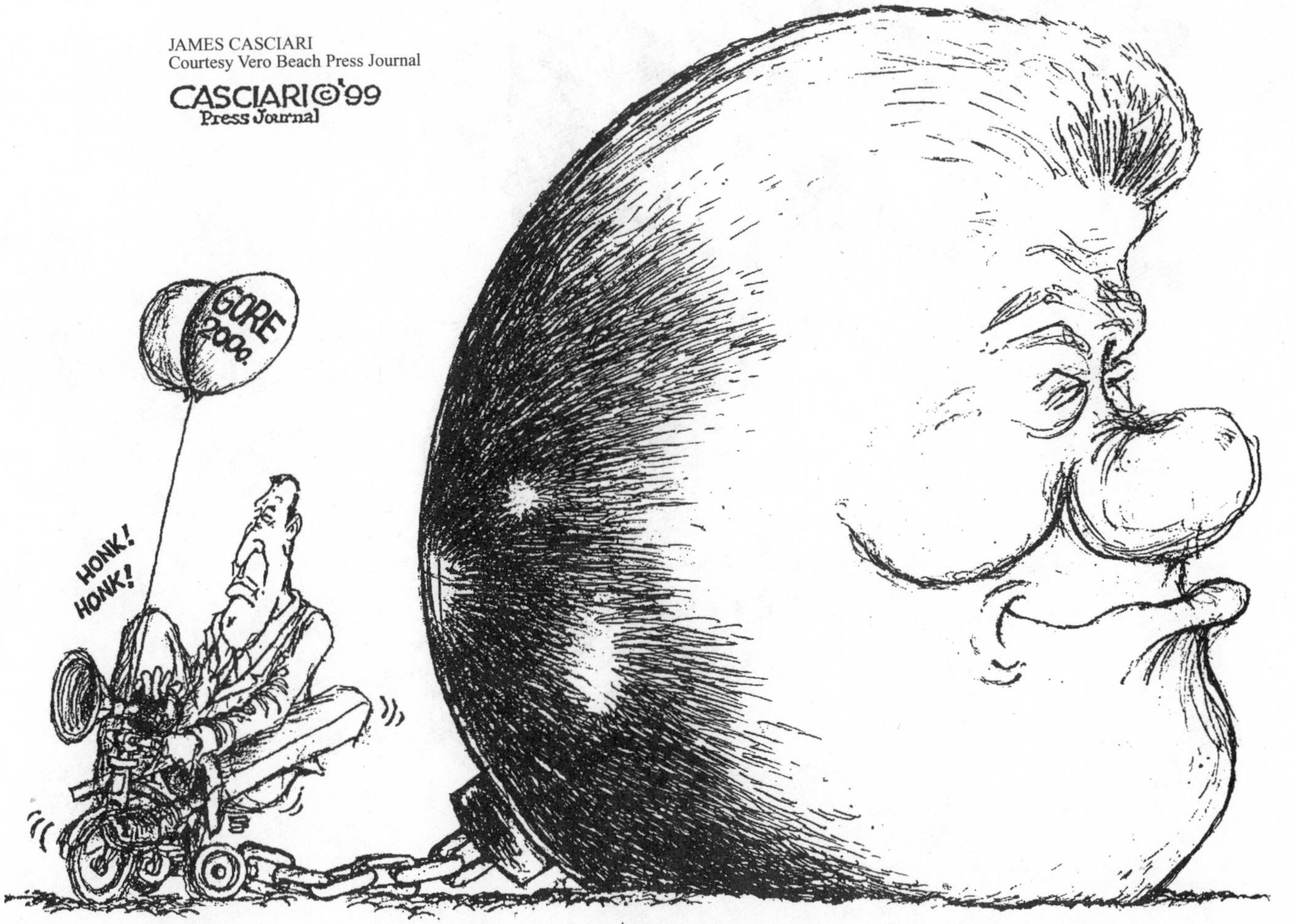
CASCIARI ©'99 Press Journal
GORE 2000
HONK! HONK!

LARRY WRIGHT
Courtesy Detroit News

MARSHALL RAMSEY
Courtesy Jackson Clarion-Ledger (Miss.)

JERRY HOLBERT
Courtesy Boston Herald

JEFF KOTERBA
Courtesy Omaha World-Herald

JAKE FULLER
Courtesy Gainesville Sun

BILL GARNER
Courtesy Washington Times

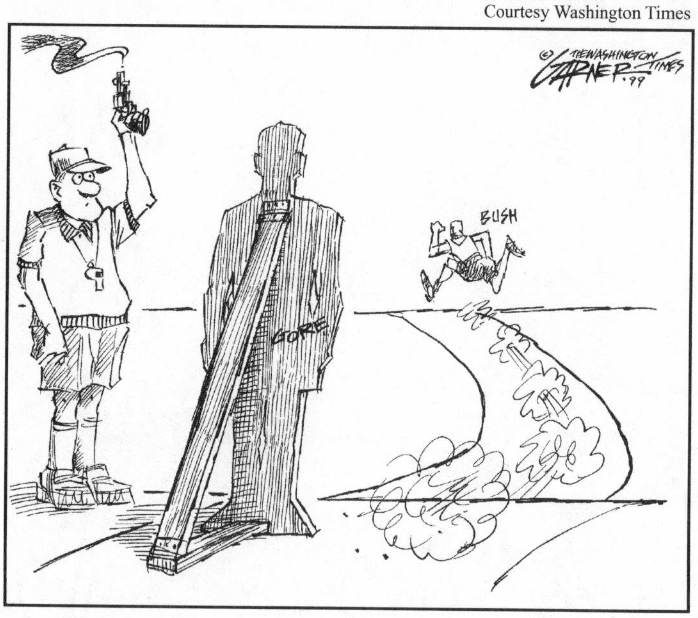
©THE WASHINGTON TIMES GARNER '99
BUSH
GORE

FRANK CAMMUSO
Courtesy Syracuse Herald-Journal

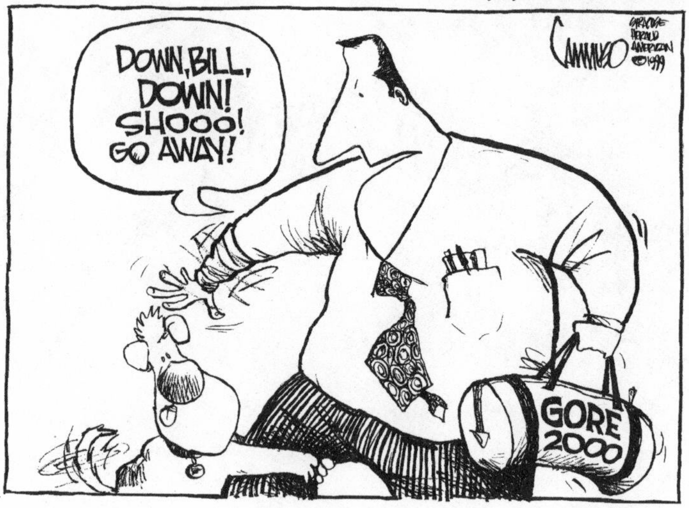
CAMMUSO ©1999
DOWN, BILL, DOWN! SHOOO! GO AWAY!
GORE 2000

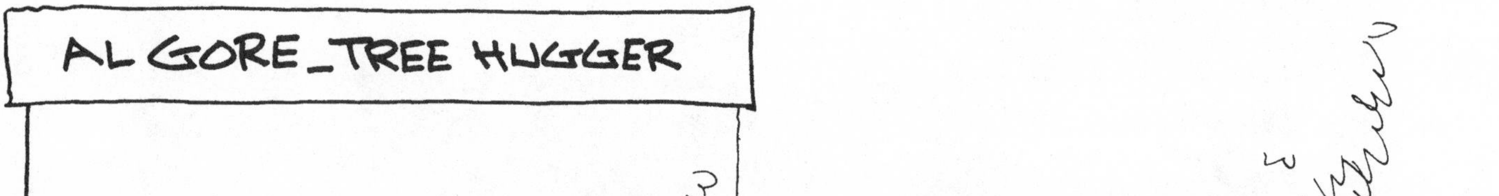
AL GORE_TREE HUGGER
HUG HUG HUG
HUG HUG
CLICK CLICK CLICK
BILL + AL
THERE HE GOES__OFF TO HUG ANOTHER TREE, NO DOUBT-
DANIEL ©THE KNOXVILLE NEWS-SENTINEL

CHARLIE DANIEL
Courtesy Knoxville News-Sentinel

REX BABIN
Courtesy Sacramento Bee

JON RICHARDS
Courtesy Santa Fe Reporter

CHIP BOK
Courtesy Akron Beacon Journal

PAUL CONRAD
Courtesy Los Angeles Times Syndicate

DEAD IN THE WOMB

JACK OHMAN
Courtesy The Oregonian

Congress

Congress dragged its feet on campaign finance reform and on term limits. Nothing was done on either. President Clinton vetoed the Republicans' $792 billion tax cut, contending that it was much too large. Both parties went on a spending spree that completely obliterated the $38 billion fiscal year 2000 surplus.

Certain to be a campaign issue was the Senate's rejection of the proposed nuclear test ban treaty, which would have barred nuclear weapons tests worldwide and established a monitoring network.

President Clinton invoked executive privilege regarding his decision to grant clemency to 16 Puerto Rican terrorists in New York while wife Hillary was campaigning there for the U.S. Senate. After six months of investigation, Rep. Christopher Cox's House committee released a 700-page report accusing China of "targeting militarily sensitive technology" developed by the United States. The report concluded that China had done so "in a deliberate and sustained effort that extends over several decades."

The controversial independent counsel law, under which Ken Starr operated, was quietly allowed to die. Congress gave its okay for public schools to display the Ten Commandments.

ED GAMBLE
Courtesy Florida Times-Union

REX BABIN
Courtesy Albany Times Union (N.Y.)

JOHN TREVER
Courtesy Albuquerque Journal

MIKE PETERS
Courtesy Dayton Daily News

MIKE LUCKOVICH
Courtesy Atlanta Constitution

JIM BERRY
Courtesy NEA

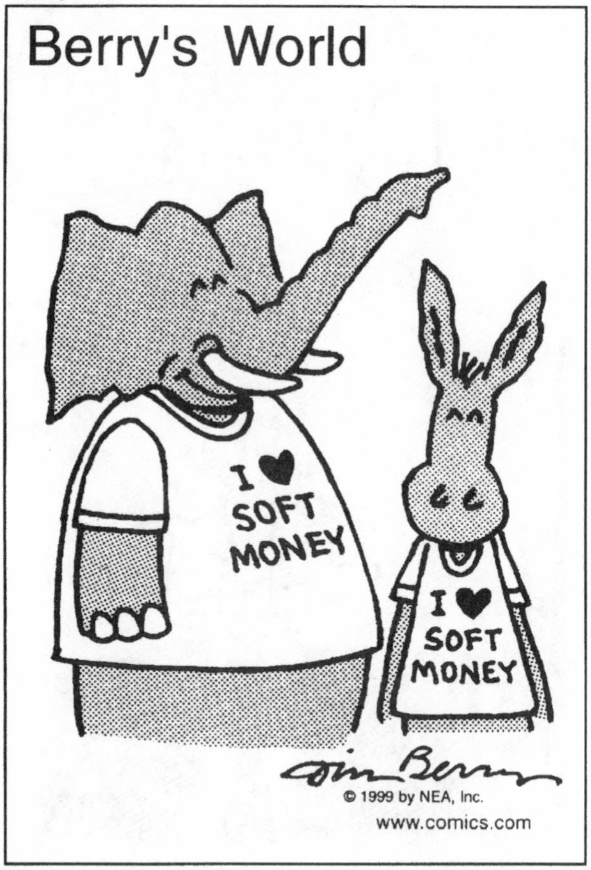
Berry's World
I ♥ SOFT MONEY
I ♥ SOFT MONEY
Jim Berry
© 1999 by NEA, Inc.
www.comics.com

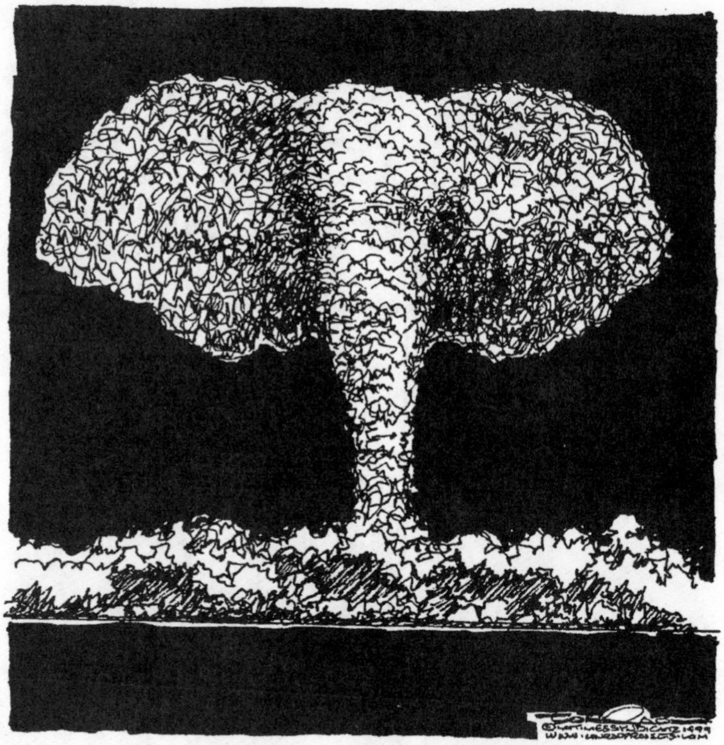

PAUL CONRAD
Courtesy Los Angeles Times Syndicate

ETTA HULME
Courtesy Fort Worth Star-Telegram

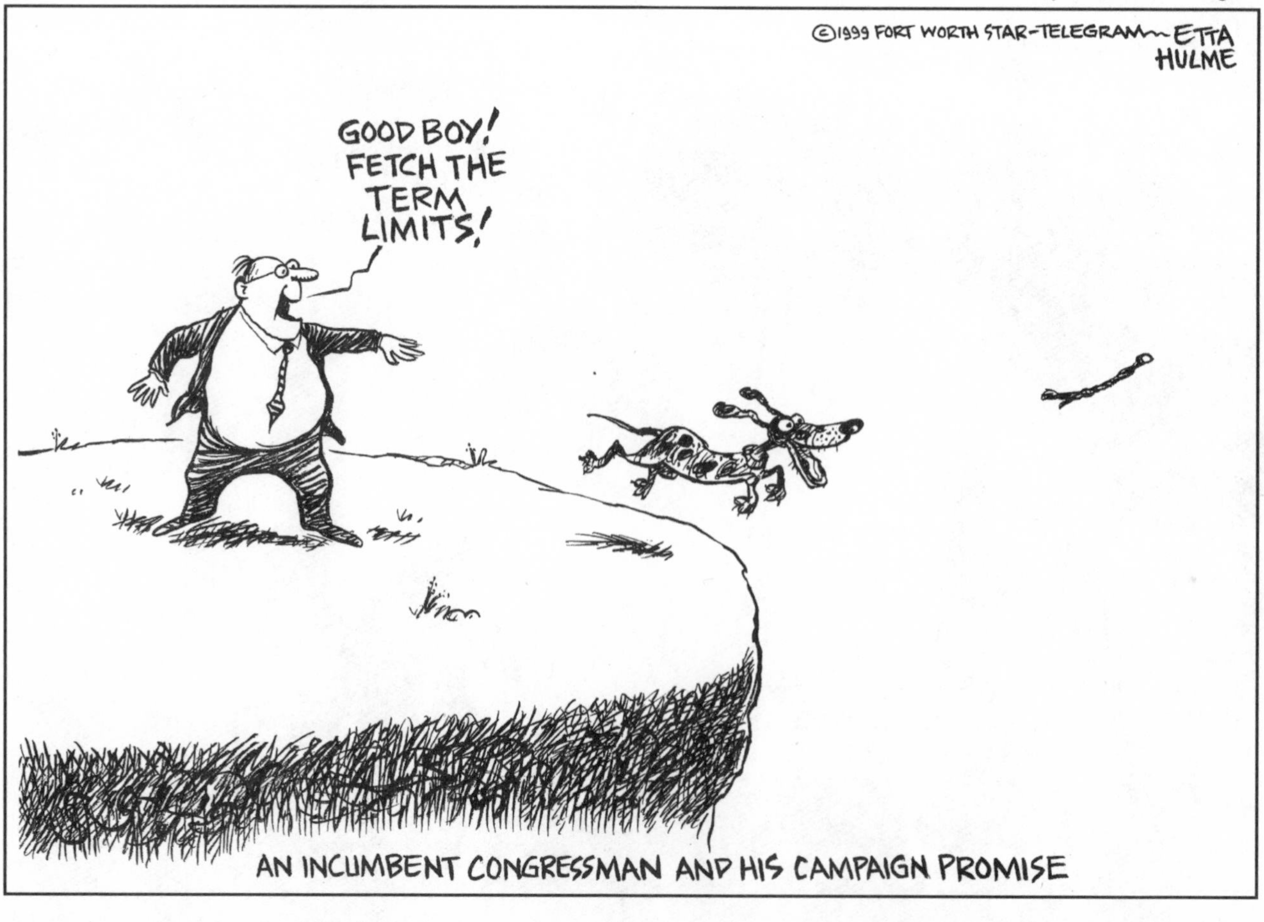
©1999 FORT WORTH STAR-TELEGRAM ETTA HULME
GOOD BOY! FETCH THE TERM LIMITS!
AN INCUMBENT CONGRESSMAN AND HIS CAMPAIGN PROMISE

BEN SARGENT
Courtesy Austin American-Statesman

ED STEIN
Courtesy Rocky Mountain News

BOB GORRELL
Courtesy Creators Syndicate
©1999 CREATORS SYNDICATE INC.
WWW.CREATORS.COM
GORRELL

BOB LANG
Courtesy The News-Sentinel (Ind.)

PETER DUNLAP-SHOHL
Courtesy Anchorage Daily News

DEFACING THE CHURCH-STATE WALL

ROB ROGERS
Courtesy Pittsburgh Post-Gazette

DREW SHENEMAN
Courtesy Newark Star-Ledger

SUPERPOWER

ROY PETERSON
Courtesy Vancouver Sun

BEN SARGENT
Courtesy Austin American-Statesman

STEPHEN TEMPLETON
Courtesy Fayetteville Observer (N.C.)

NEIL GRAHAME
Courtesy Spencer Newspapers

JAMES CASCIARI
Courtesy Vero Beach Press Journal

JACK HIGGINS
Courtesy Chicago Sun-Times

♪ ... GAVE PROOF THROUGH THE NIGHT THAT OUR FLAG WAS STILL THERE ...

RICK McKEE
Courtesy Augusta Chronicle

Foreign Affairs

Following reports that sensitive missile technology had been given to China by the Clinton Administration, the Senate launched an investigation. It was discovered that the Chinese had obtained substantial information on advanced U.S. thermonuclear weapons from U.S. weapons laboratories, and that the information transfer was continuing.

Ethnic fighting in Kosovo intensified, and NATO ordered air strikes against the Serb forces. It marked the first time NATO had ever attacked a sovereign power. A United Nations tribunal formally indicted Yugoslav President Slobodan Milosevic for war crimes, the first time a head of state had ever been so charged. Russia continued to be beset by widespread corruption, and Boris Yeltsin continued to show evidence of drunkenness and erratic behavior before resigning December 31. Russian forces attacked Chechnya in September in an attempt to wipe out Islamic resistance in the breakaway republic.

After two bloody months of fighting, East Timor was granted independence by Indonesia. Israeli prime minister Benjamin Netanyahu was unseated by former general and war hero Ehud Barak. Barak's primary objective of securing peace in the Middle East was pursued vigorously, but real peace remained elusive. China made veiled threats toward Taiwan and reminded the world that it, too, possesses the neutron bomb.

JEFF MacNELLY
Courtesy Chicago Tribune

STEVE McBRIDE
Courtesy Independence Daily Reporter

MIKE THOMPSON
Courtesy Detroit Free Press

KEVIN KALLAUGHER
Courtesy Baltimore Sun

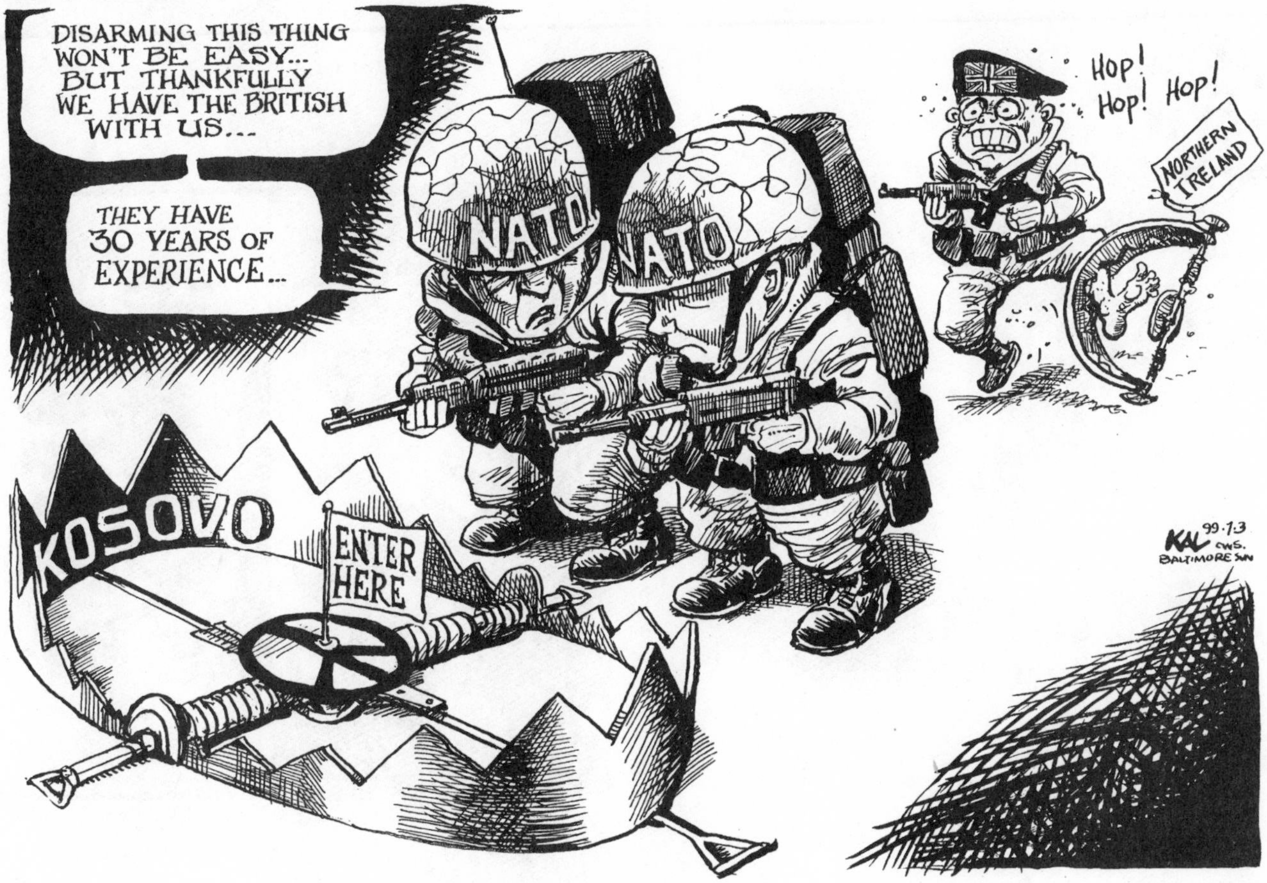
DISARMING THIS THING WON'T BE EASY... BUT THANKFULLY WE HAVE THE BRITISH WITH US...
THEY HAVE 30 YEARS OF EXPERIENCE...
Hop! Hop! Hop!
NORTHERN IRELAND
NATO
NATO
KOSOVO
ENTER HERE
KAL 99.1.3 CWS. BALTIMORE SUN

TIM HARTMAN
Courtesy North Hills News Record (Pa.)

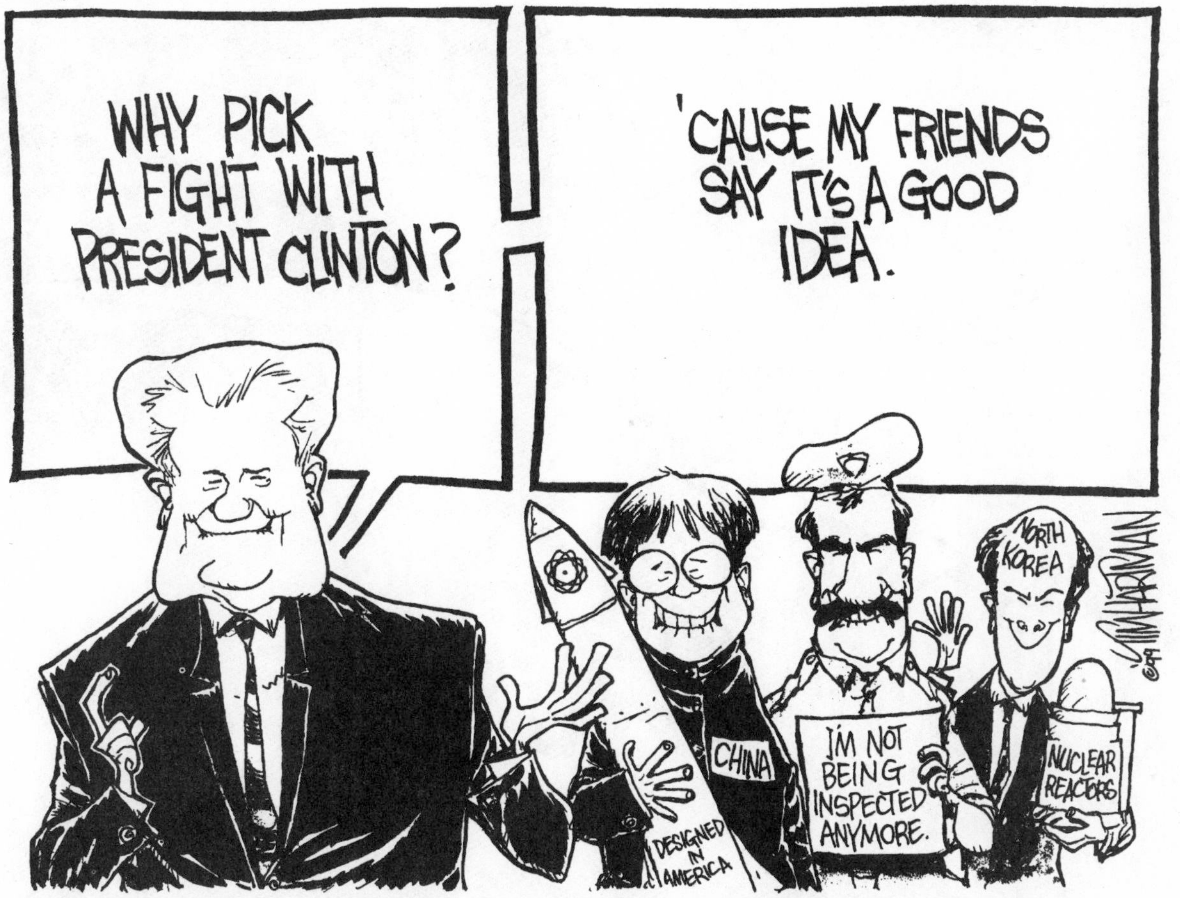
WHY PICK A FIGHT WITH PRESIDENT CLINTON?
'CAUSE MY FRIENDS SAY IT'S A GOOD IDEA.
NORTH KOREA
CHINA
I'M NOT BEING INSPECTED ANYMORE.
NUCLEAR REACTORS
DESIGNED IN AMERICA
TIM HARTMAN

FRED CURATOLO
Courtesy Edmonton Sun (Alberta)

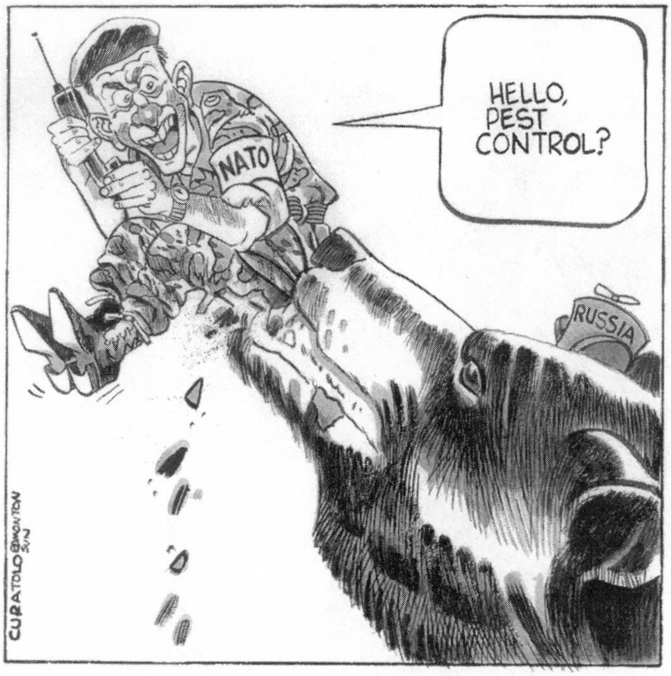
HELLO, PEST CONTROL?
NATO
RUSSIA
CURATOLO EDMONTON SUN

GUY BADEAUX
Courtesy Le Droit (Ottawa)

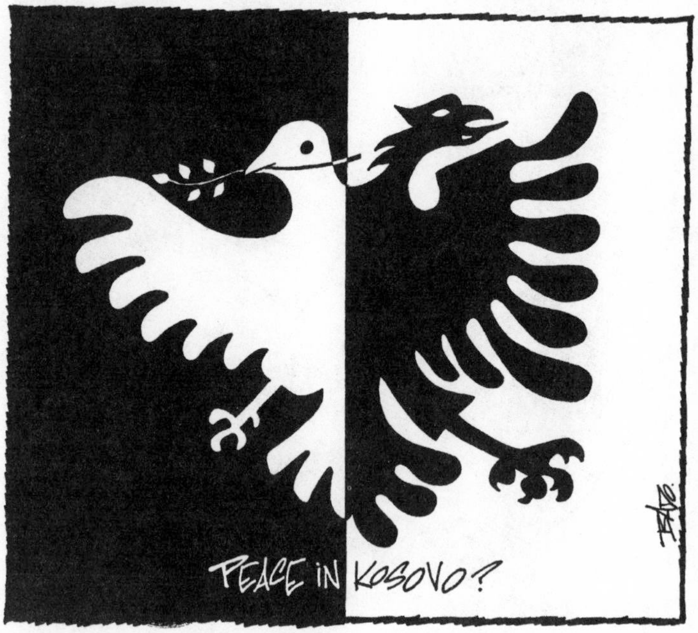
PEACE IN KOSOVO?

MIKE KEEFE
Courtesy Denver Post

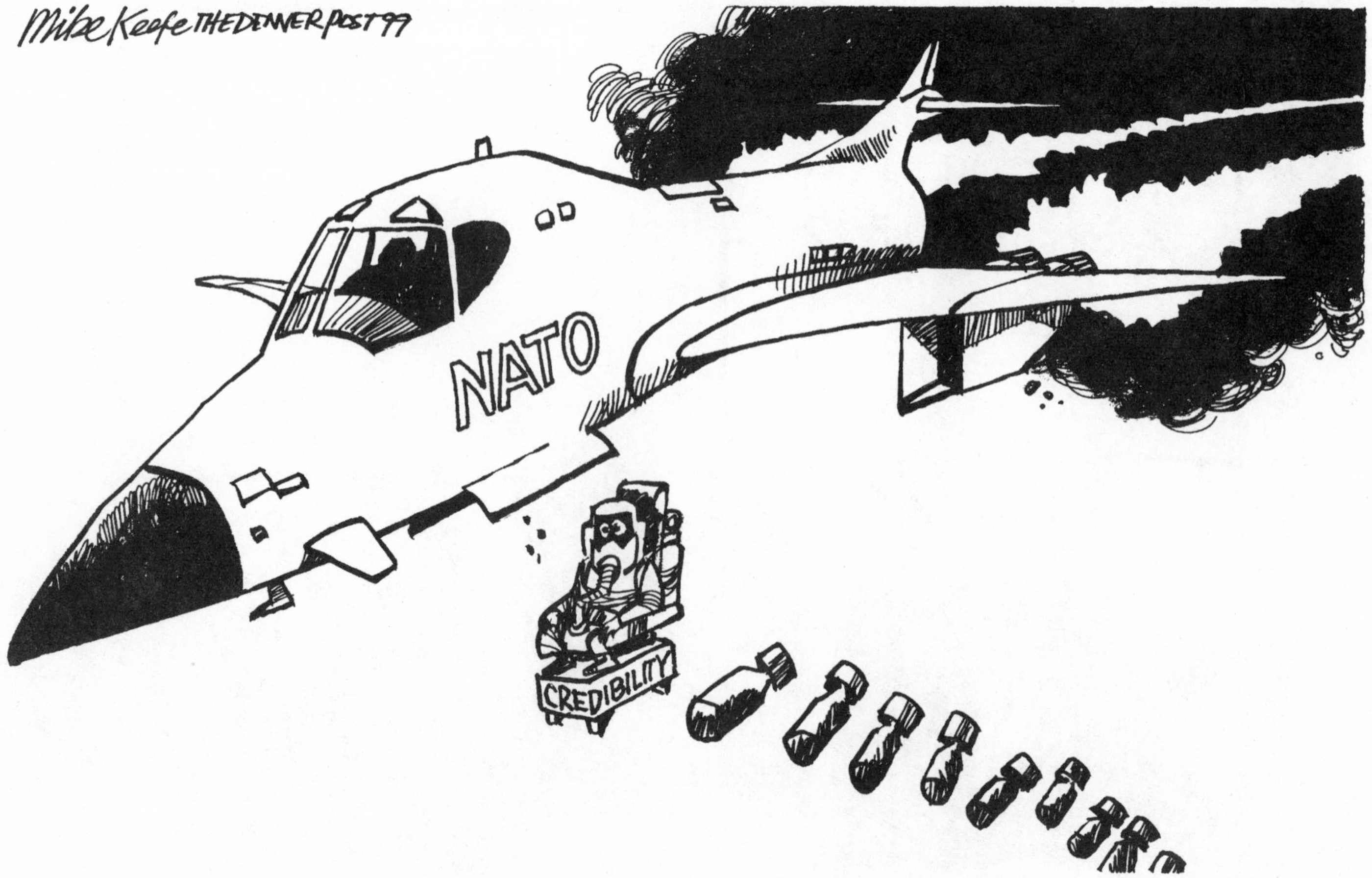
Mike Keefe THE DENVER POST 99
NATO
CREDIBILITY

JAMES McCLOSKEY
Courtesy Staunton Daily News Leader

The Russian Method of Carefully Avoiding Harm to Innocent Civilians

JEFF DANZIGER
Courtesy Los Angeles Times Syndicate

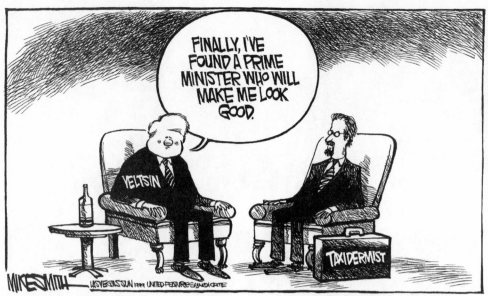

MIKE SMITH
Courtesy United Features Syndicate

PAUL CONRAD
Courtesy Los Angeles Times Syndicate

GARY BROOKINS
Courtesy Richmond Times-Dispatch

BILL GARNER
Courtesy Washington Times

PETER DUNLAP-SHOHL
Courtesy Anchorage Daily News

Berry's World

JIM BERRY
Courtesy NEA

J. R. ROSE
Courtesy Byrd Newspapers

GEORGE DANBY
Courtesy Bangor Daily News

JACK HIGGINS
Courtesy Chicago Sun-Times

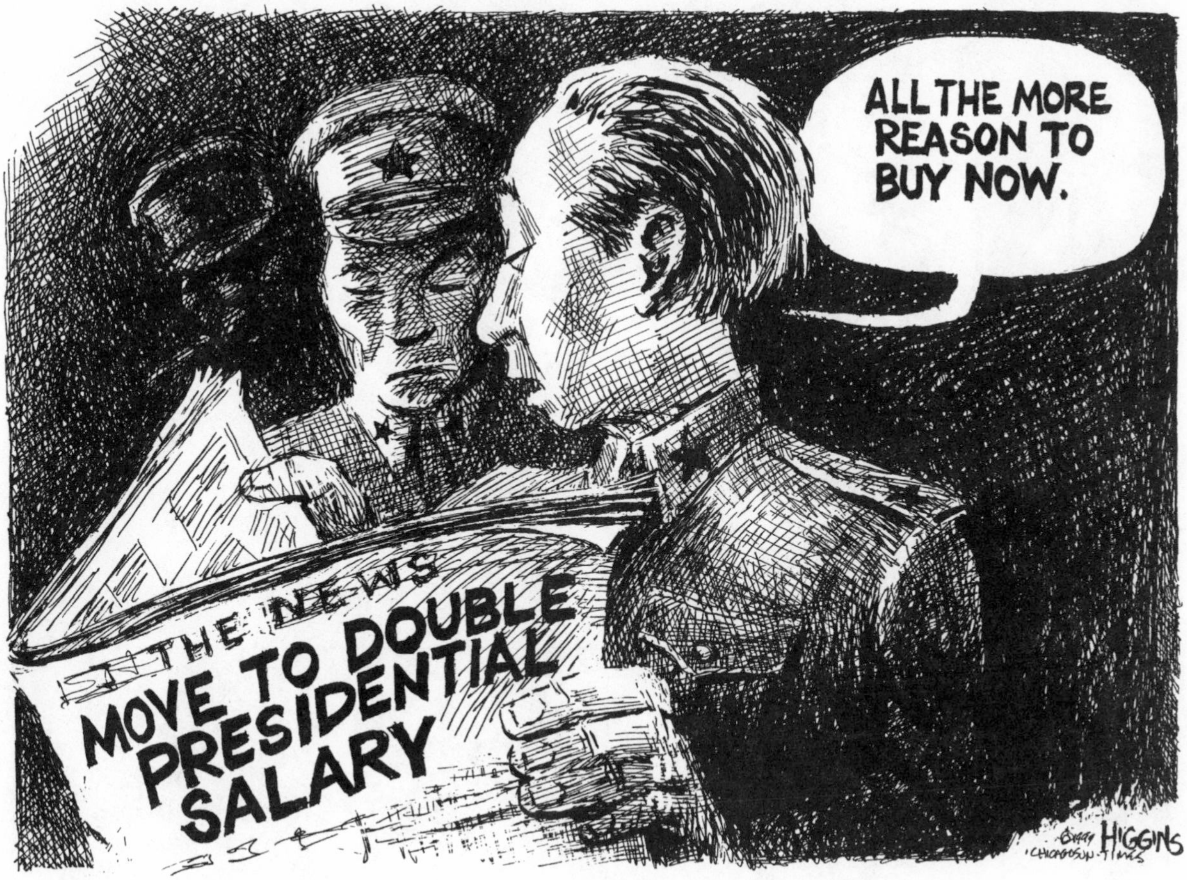
ALL THE MORE REASON TO BUY NOW.
THE NEWS
MOVE TO DOUBLE PRESIDENTIAL SALARY
HIGGINS

JERRY HOLBERT
Courtesy Boston Herald

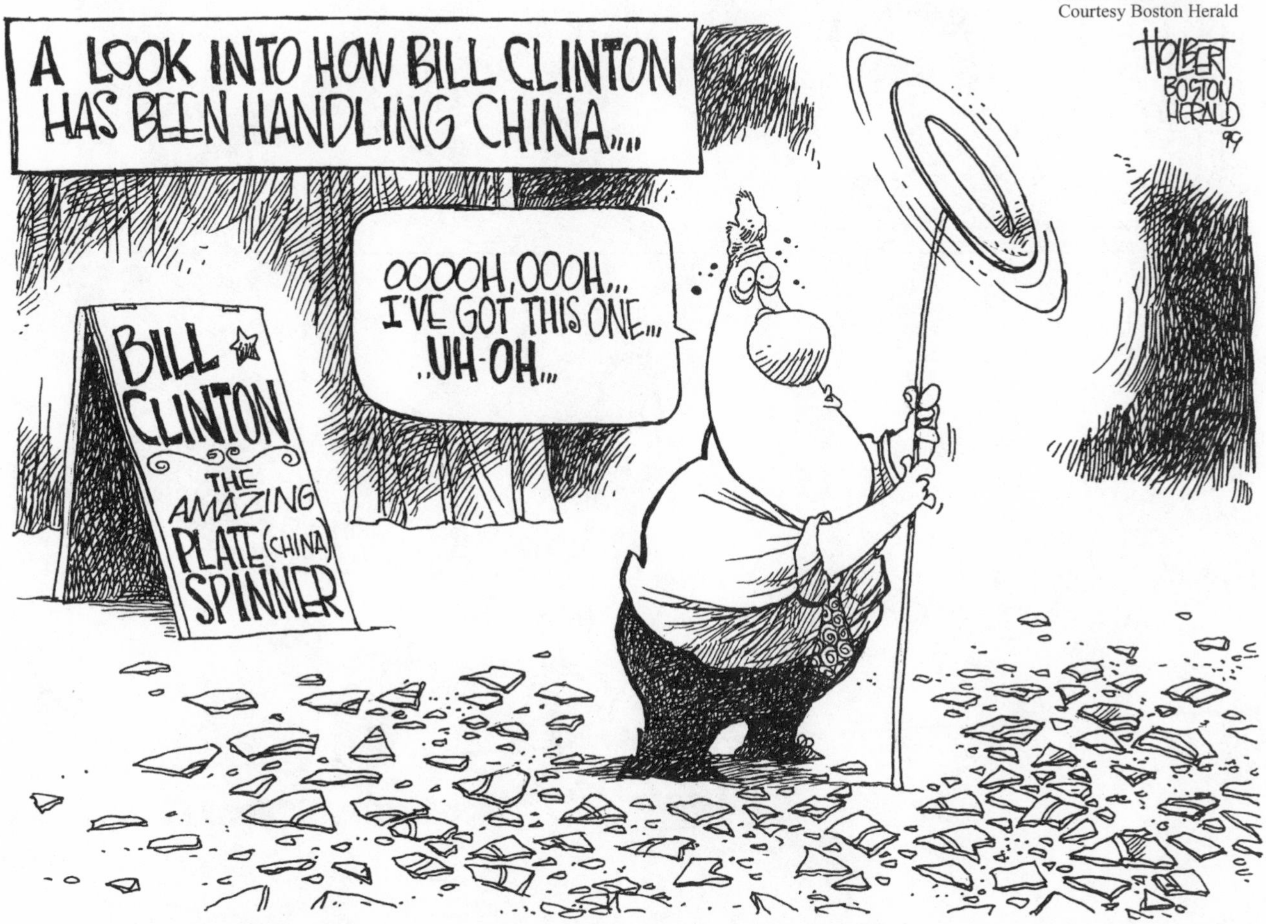
A LOOK INTO HOW BILL CLINTON HAS BEEN HANDLING CHINA....
HOLBERT BOSTON HERALD
OOOOH, OOOH... I'VE GOT THIS ONE... ..UH-OH...
BILL CLINTON
THE AMAZING PLATE (CHINA) SPINNER

DANI AGUILA
Courtesy Filipino Reporter

BARBARA BRANDON-CROFT
Courtesy Universal Press Syndicate

SIGNE WILKINSON
Courtesy Philadelphia Daily News

CHUCK ASAY
Courtesy Colorado Springs Gazette-Telegraph

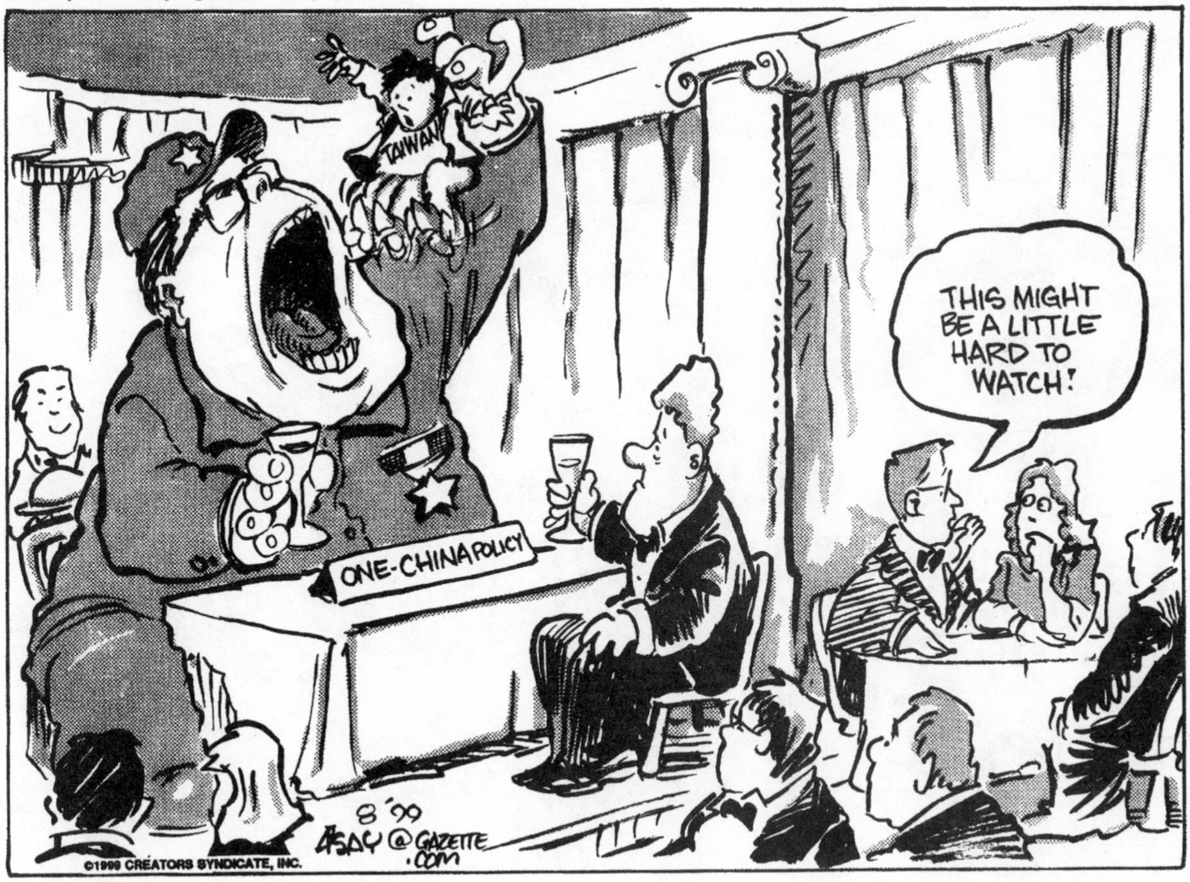
TAIWAN
THIS MIGHT BE A LITTLE HARD TO WATCH!
ONE-CHINA POLICY
8 '99
ASAY @GAZETTE.COM
©1999 CREATORS SYNDICATE, INC.

STEVE McBRIDE
Courtesy Independence Daily Reporter

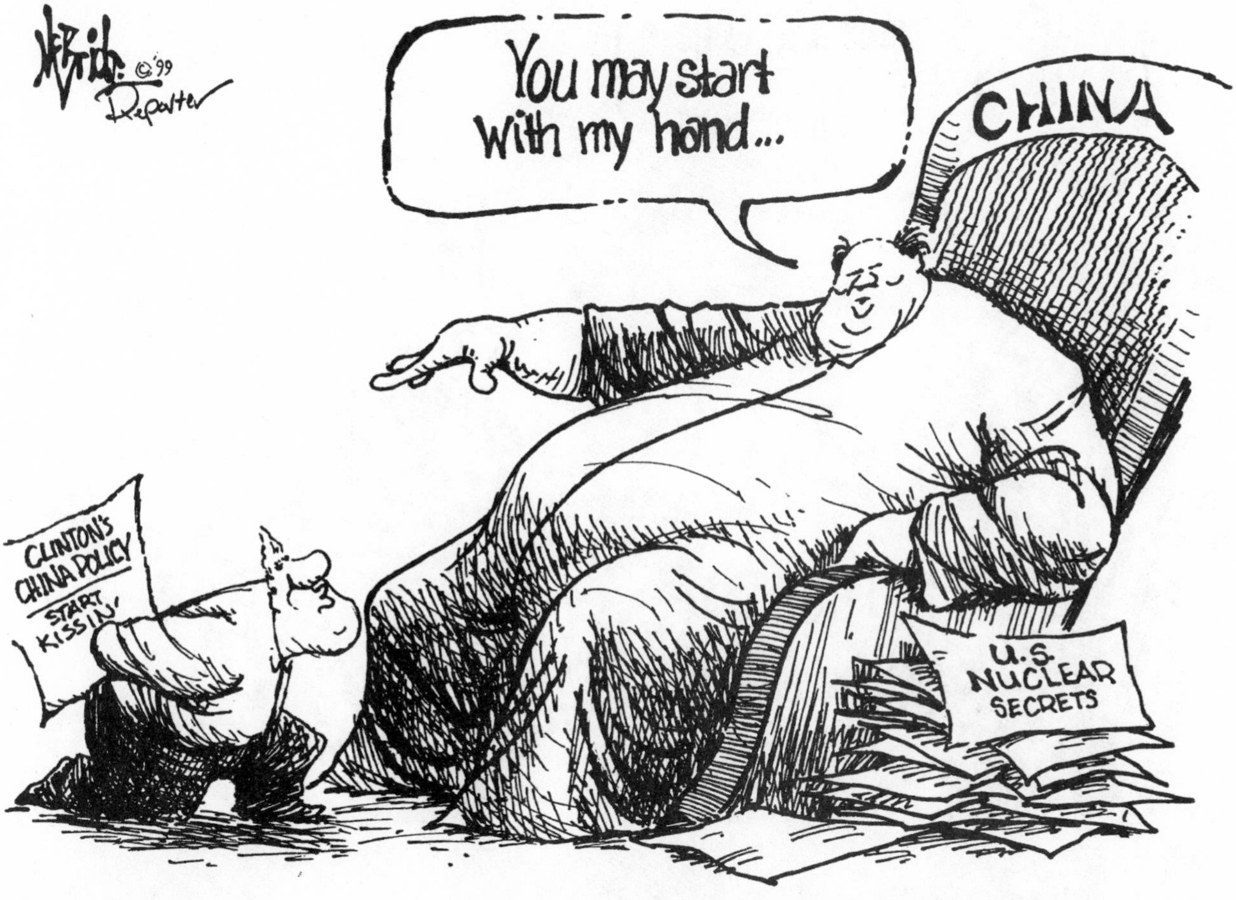
McBride ©'99 Reporter
You may start with my hand...
CHINA
CLINTON'S CHINA POLICY
START KISSIN'
U.S. NUCLEAR SECRETS

DENNIS DRAUGHON
Courtesy Scranton Times

EUGENE PAYNE
Courtesy Charlotte Observer

Everything Under Control in Moscow

93

DAVE GRANLUND
Courtesy Metrowest Daily News

ERIC SMITH
Courtesy Annapolis Capital-Gazette

GARY VARVEL
Courtesy Indianapolis Star

MARSHALL RAMSEY
Courtesy Jackson Clarion-Ledger (Miss.)

DAVID HORSEY
Courtesy Seattle Post-Intelligencer

"THEY TELL ME I SHOULD FEEL GOOD ABOUT THE COMPETITION!"

ROBERT ARIAIL
Courtesy The State (S.C.)

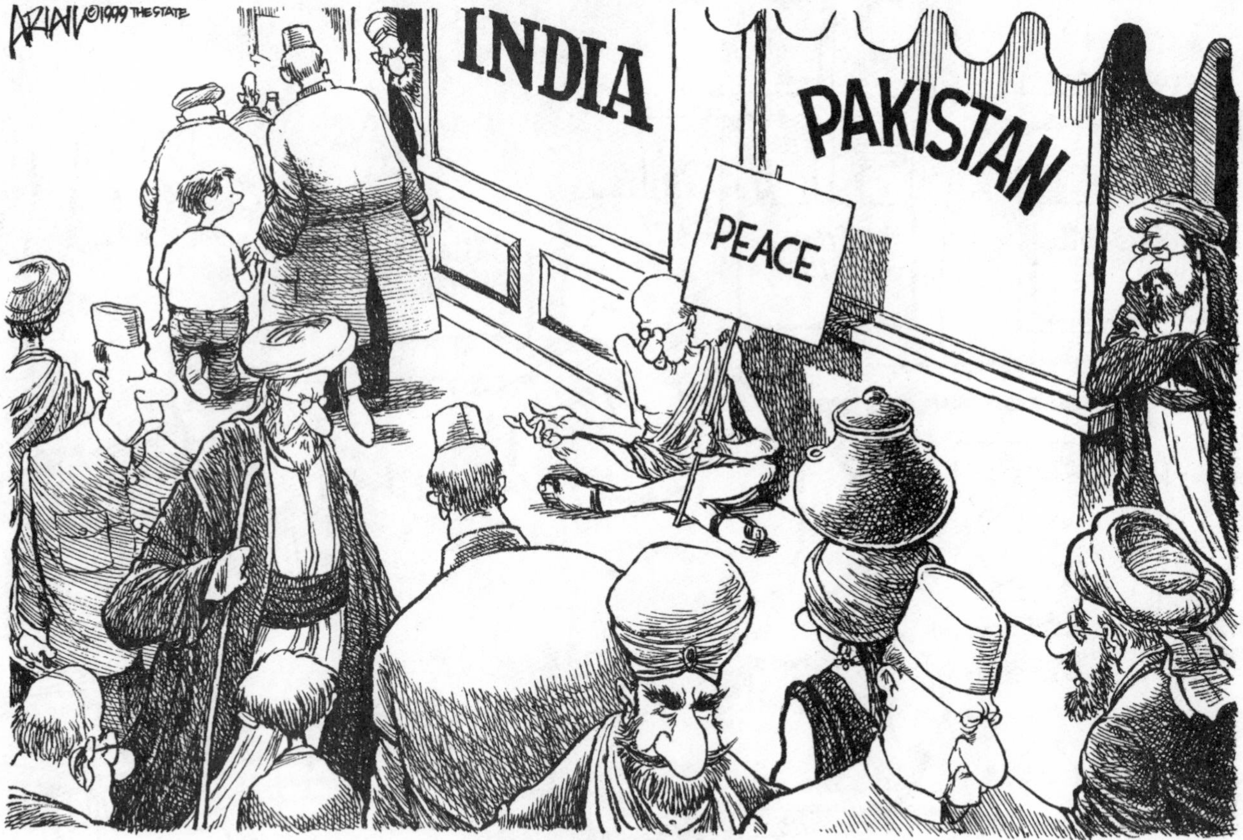
ARIAIL ©1999 THE STATE
INDIA
PAKISTAN
PEACE

"THE UNTOUCHABLE"

KEVIN KALLAUGHER
Courtesy Baltimore Sun

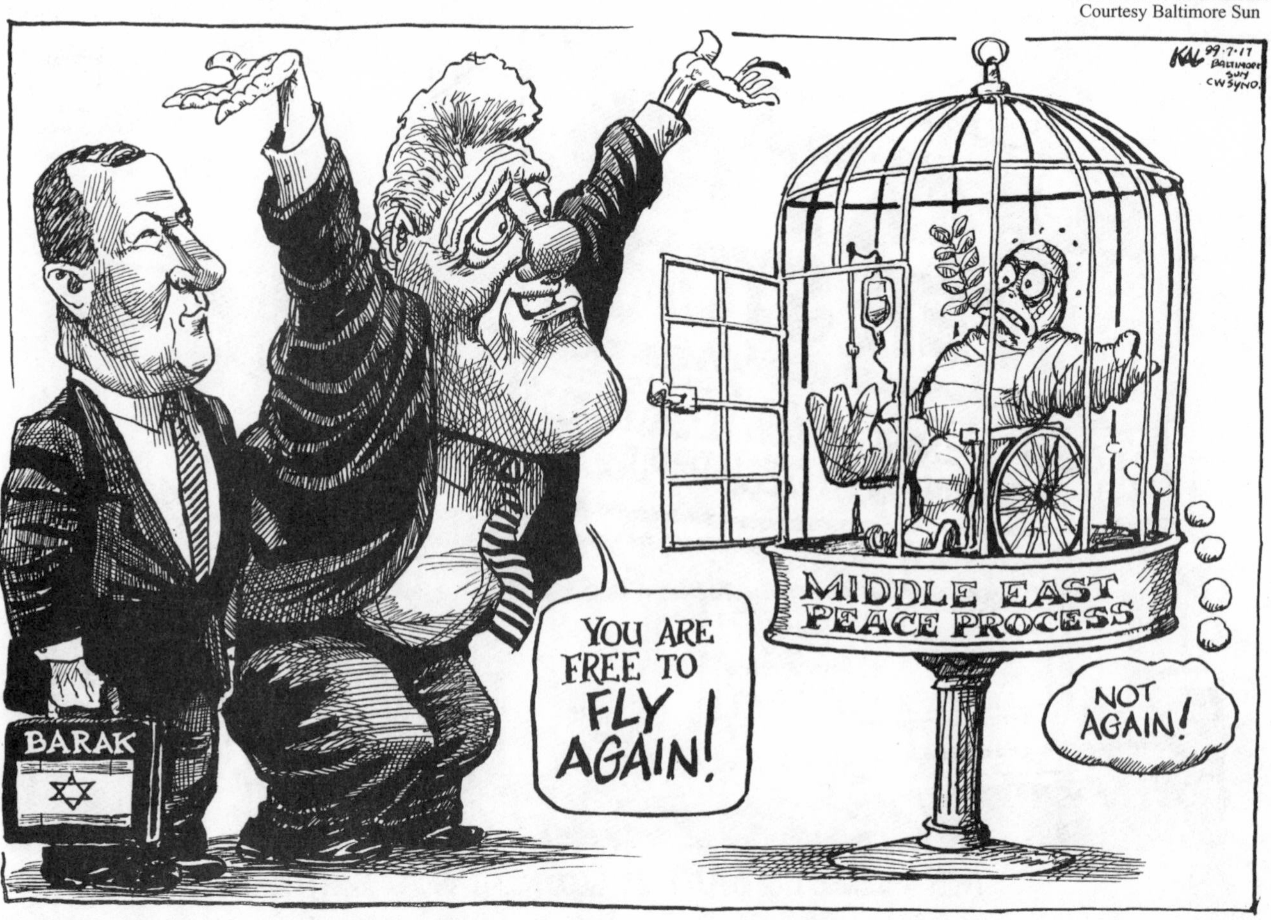
KAL 99.7.17 BALTIMORE SUN CW SYND.
YOU ARE FREE TO FLY AGAIN!
MIDDLE EAST PEACE PROCESS
NOT AGAIN!
BARAK

VICTIMS WHEN NATO BOMBS MISS THEIR TARGETS...

...AND WHEN SERBIAN ONES HIT THEIRS.

JOHN KOVALIC
Courtesy Shetland Productions

JOHN BRANCH
Courtesy San Antonio Express-News

ERIC SMITH
Courtesy Annapolis Capital-Gazette

RICHARD CROWSON
Courtesy Wichita Eagle

BEANIE DRAGON

JIMMY MARGULIES
Courtesy Hackensack Record

MARGULIES
©1999 THE RECORD
www.bergen.com/margulies

98

BILL GARNER
Courtesy Washington Times

Highest Mission

JEFF DANZIGER
Courtesy Los Angeles Times Syndicate

JOHN MARSHALL
Courtesy Binghamton Press & Sun-Bulletin

CLAY BENNETT
Courtesy Christian Science Monitor

The Economy

Confounding most experts, U.S. economic output continued its record expansion during 1999. Federal Resereve Chairman Alan Greenspan kept a wary eye out for signs of inflation because of the surging money supply and rising commodity prices. At the same time, unemployment in the tight job market plunged to all-time lows. The Federal Reserve raised interest rates three times during the year in an effort to keep inflation in check. Despite the economy's sustained growth, many workers were feeling insecure because of mergers and changes in the business world.

Farmers did not fare well during the year. Small farmers remained an endangered species, their total having dropped nearly 5 million since the 1930s. In the past, farmers could rely on strong animal or dairy prices when grain prices fell, or vice versa. But in 1999 all prime agriculture products were in the doldrums.

Gasoline prices at the pump took a hefty jump as the price of crude oil climbed to its highest level since the war in the Persian Gulf. The use of gasoline in the U.S. is boosted by the fact that there are increasingly larger numbers of sports utility vehicles on the road, requiring more fuel than regular cars.

CHARLIE DANIEL
Courtesy Knoxville News-Sentinel

KIRK ANDERSON
Courtesy St. Paul Pioneer Press

DENNIS DRAUGHON
Courtesy Scranton Times

MILT PRIGGEE
Courtesy Spokane Spokesman-Review

102

ROGER SCHILLERSTROM
Courtesy Crain Communications

ED STEIN
Courtesy Rocky Mountain News

"Too bad you only have nine lives . . . I'm going to live forever!"

ARLINGTON MORNING NEWS

WILLIAM L. FLINT
Courtesy Arlington Morning News

STEVE LINDSTROM
Courtesy Duluth News-Tribune

ED FISCHER
Courtesy Agri-News

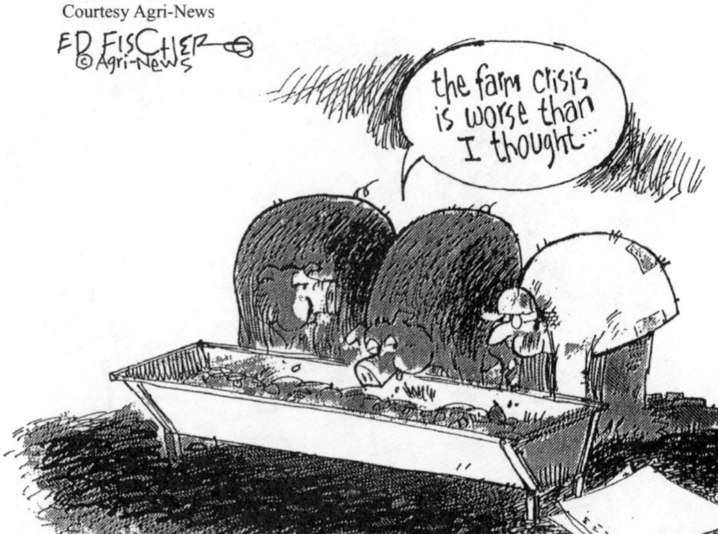

ED FISCHER
© Agri-News
the farm crisis is worse than I thought...

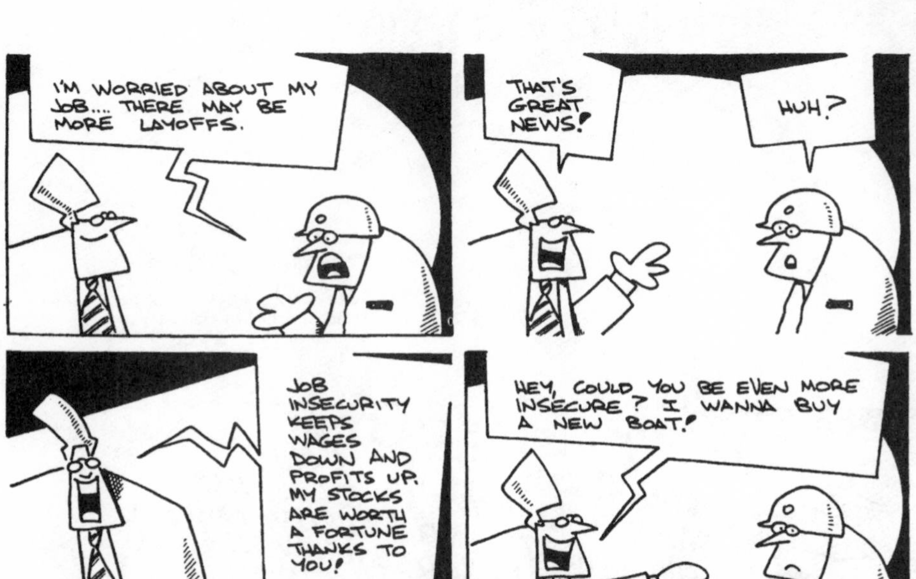

I'M WORRIED ABOUT MY JOB.... THERE MAY BE MORE LAYOFFS.
THAT'S GREAT NEWS!
HUH?
JOB INSECURITY KEEPS WAGES DOWN AND PROFITS UP. MY STOCKS ARE WORTH A FORTUNE THANKS TO YOU!
HEY, COULD YOU BE EVEN MORE INSECURE? I WANNA BUY A NEW BOAT!
BATEMAN ©99 Batetoon@aol.com
http://members.aol.com/batetoon/

SCOTT BATEMAN
Courtesy North American Syndicate

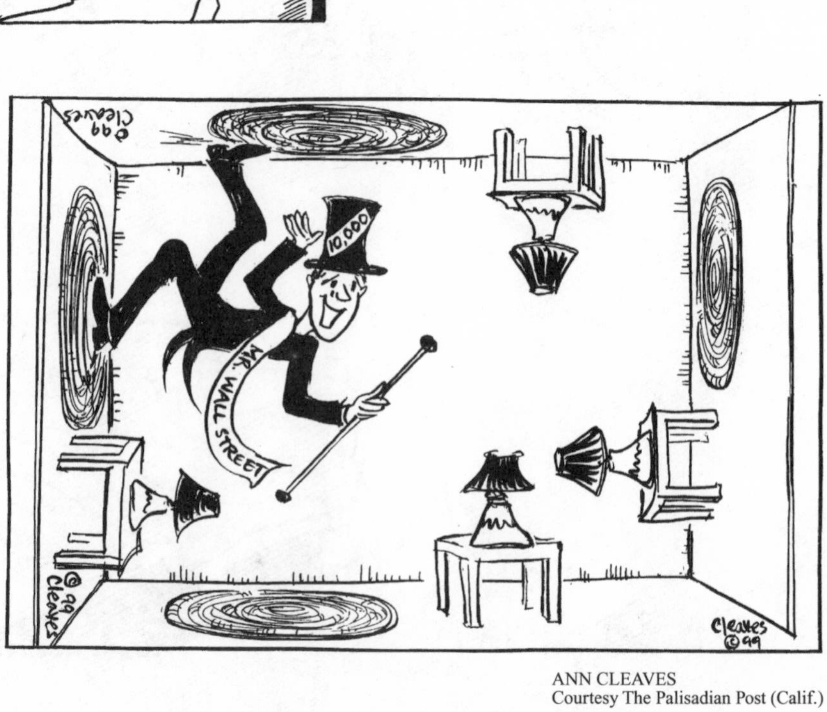

10,000
MR. WALL STREET
CLEAVES ©99

ANN CLEAVES
Courtesy The Palisadian Post (Calif.)

GEORGE DANBY
Courtesy Bangor Daily News

DOUGLAS REGALIA
Courtesy Contra Costa Times

JEFF MacNELLY
Courtesy Chicago Tribune

DREW SHENEMAN
Courtesy Newark Star-Ledger

SCOTT STANTIS
Courtesy Birmingham News

Society

Senseless violence continued across the country during 1999. Mass shootings occurred at a church in Fort Worth, Texas, a day-care center in Los Angeles, a business in Alabama, a stock brokerage in Atlanta, a boat yard in Seattle, and a high school in Colorado. It was a year of grief and sadness for countless citizens.

The long-awaited sequel to *Star Wars,* called *The Phantom Menace,* appeared in movie theaters across the country as huge crowds flocked to view it. Commercialism took over, and the nation was flooded with Star Wars mementoes.

As the millennium approached and Y2K concerns increased, society seemed beset by fear of the future. In November, in an effort to reassure the populace, President Clinton announced that 99 percent of all governmental functions were prepared for the new millennium and that Y2K no longer posed a major threat.

Racism still reared its ugly head periodically, and hate crimes continued to occur from time to time. There were reports that some law enforcement officers were stopping motorists as a result of profiling—based on drivers' skin color or appearance. Many adults were still trying to understand why sizeable numbers of teenagers seemed violence-prone and still others were turning to suicide.

SCOTT STANTIS
Courtesy Birmingham News

JOHN SPENCER
Courtesy Philadelphia Business Journal

BARBARA BRANDON-CROFT
Courtesy Universal Press Syndicate

SIGNE WILKINSON
Courtesy Philadelphia Daily News

BOB ENGLEHART
Courtesy Hartford Courant

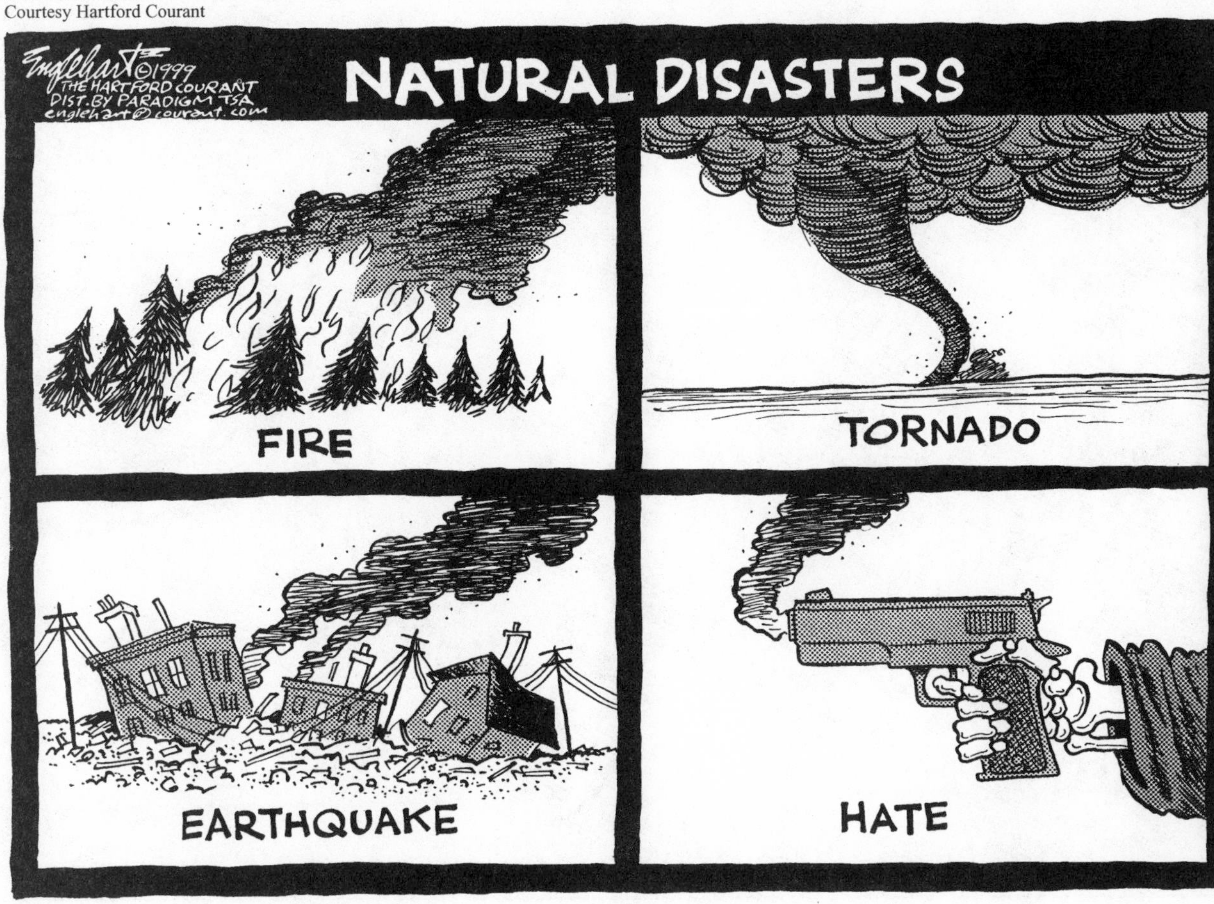
Englehart ©1999 THE HARTFORD COURANT DIST. BY PARADIGM TSA englehart@courant.com
NATURAL DISASTERS
FIRE
TORNADO
EARTHQUAKE
HATE

MICHAEL RAMIREZ
Courtesy Los Angeles Times

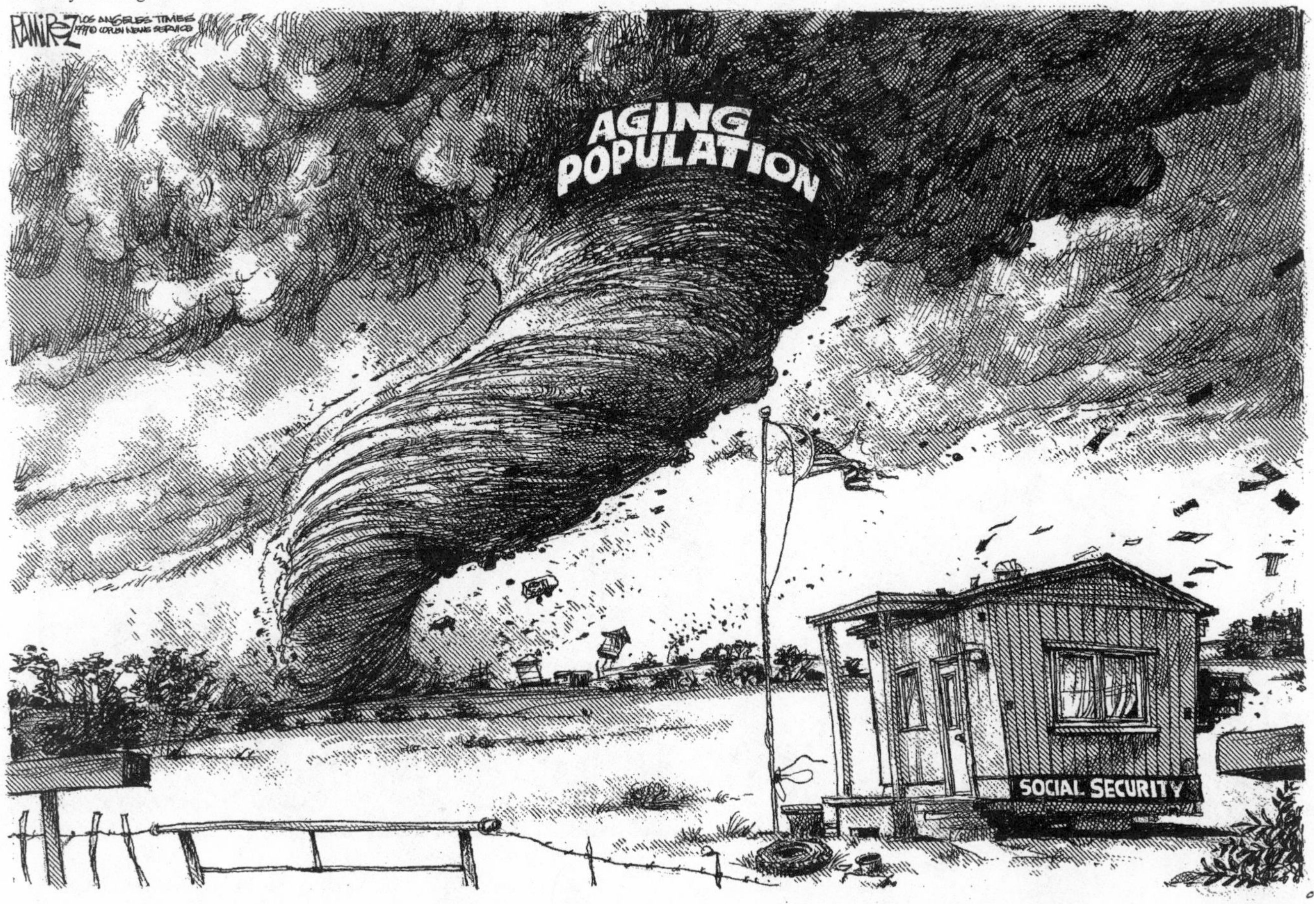
RAMIREZ
AGING POPULATION
SOCIAL SECURITY

DAVID CATROW
Courtesy Springfield News (Oh.)

"MOM, DAD—THIS IS CRYSTAL VELVET, WE MET ON the INTERNET."

JOHN MARSHALL
Courtesy Binghamton Press & Sun-Bulletin

WALT HANDELSMAN
Courtesy New Orleans Times-Picayune

JEFF STAHLER
Courtesy Cincinnati Post

113

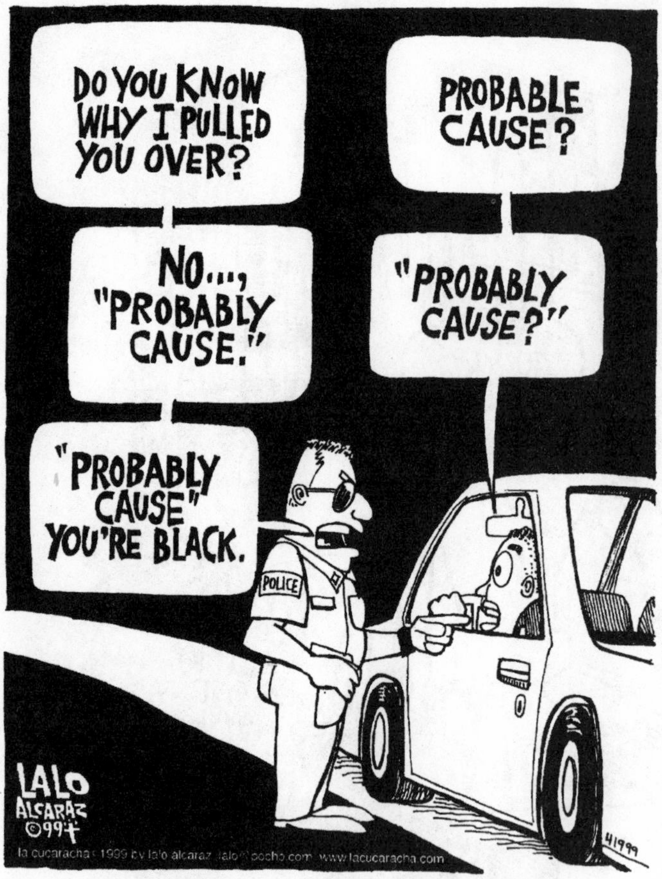
DO YOU KNOW WHY I PULLED YOU OVER?
NO..., "PROBABLY CAUSE."
"PROBABLY CAUSE" YOU'RE BLACK.
PROBABLE CAUSE?
"PROBABLY CAUSE?"
POLICE
LALO ALCARAZ ©99
4/1999

LALO ALCARAZ
Courtesy Los Angeles Weekly

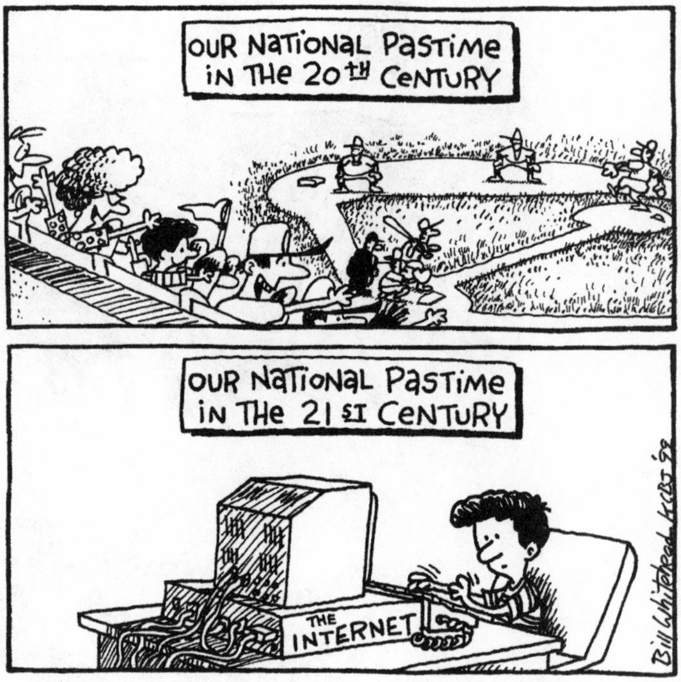
OUR NATIONAL PASTIME IN THE 20TH CENTURY
OUR NATIONAL PASTIME IN THE 21ST CENTURY
THE INTERNET
Bill Whitehead KCBJ 99

BILL WHITEHEAD
Courtesy Kansas City Business Journal

JACK OHMAN
Courtesy The Oregonian

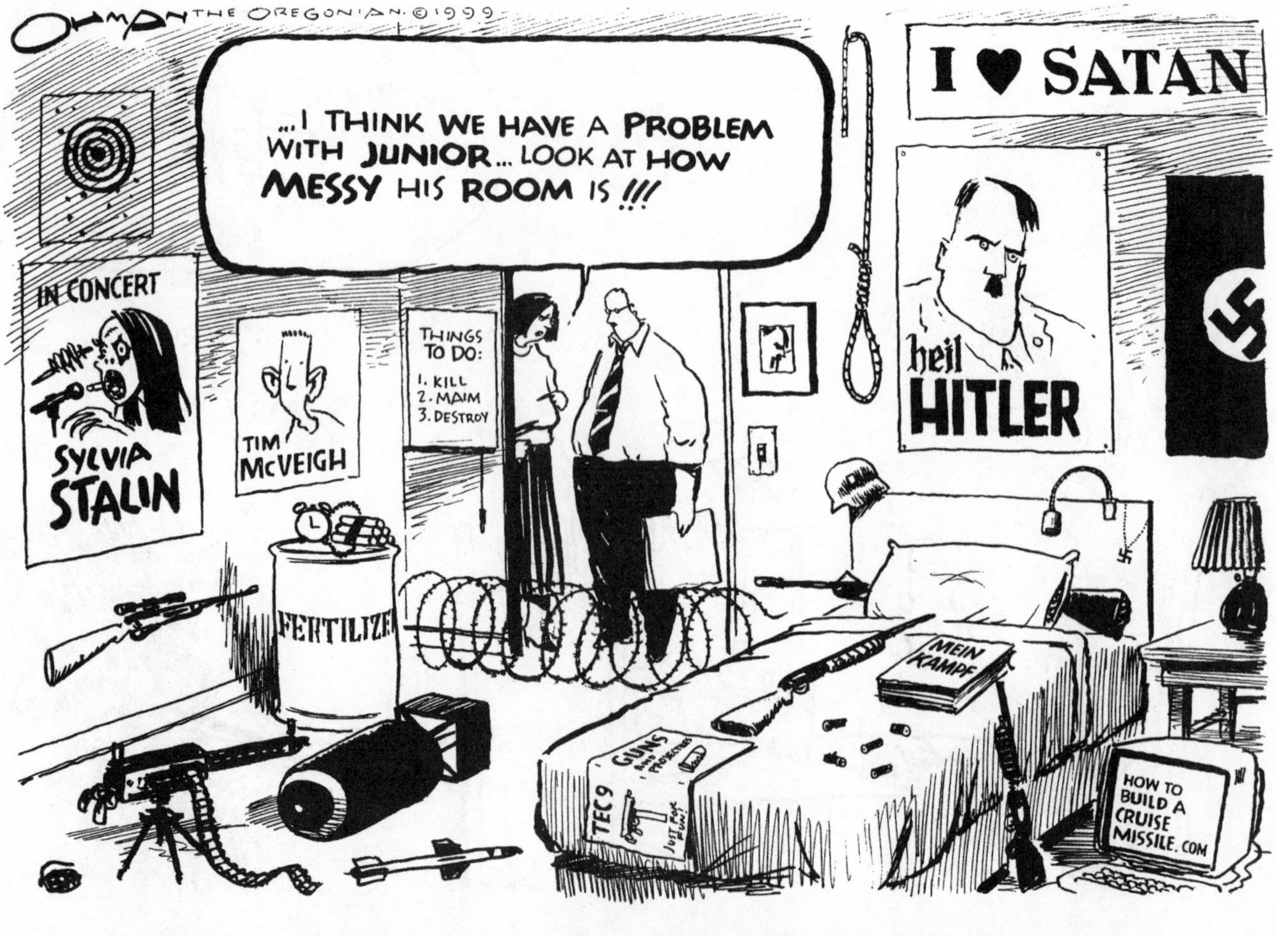
OHMAN THE OREGONIAN ©1999
...I THINK WE HAVE A PROBLEM WITH JUNIOR... LOOK AT HOW MESSY HIS ROOM IS !!!
I ♥ SATAN
IN CONCERT SYLVIA STALIN
TIM McVEIGH
THINGS TO DO: 1. KILL 2. MAIM 3. DESTROY
heil HITLER
FERTILIZE
MEIN KAMPF
GUNS
TEC 9
JUST FOR FUN
HOW TO BUILD A CRUISE MISSILE.COM

RICHARD CROWSON
Courtesy Wichita Eagle

JEFF MacNELLY
Courtesy Chicago Tribune

JIM BORGMAN
Courtesy Cincinnati Enquirer

LAZARO FRESQUET
Courtesy El Nuevo Herald (Miami)

JEFF STAHLER
Courtesy Cincinnati Post

STEPHEN TEMPLETON
Courtesy Fayetteville Observer (N.C.)

BEN SARGENT
Courtesy Austin American-Statesman

JOE HELLER
Courtesy Green Bay Press-Gazette

AMERICANS REACT TO THE CRISIS IN KOSOVO...

REX BABIN
Courtesy Albany Times Union (N.Y.)

ANNETTE BALESTERI
Courtesy Antioch Ledger-Dispatch (Calif.)

ETTA HULME
Courtesy Fort Worth Star-Telegram

DON LANDGREN, JR.
Courtesy The Landmark (Mass.)

JAMES McCLOSKEY
Courtesy Staunton Daily News Leader

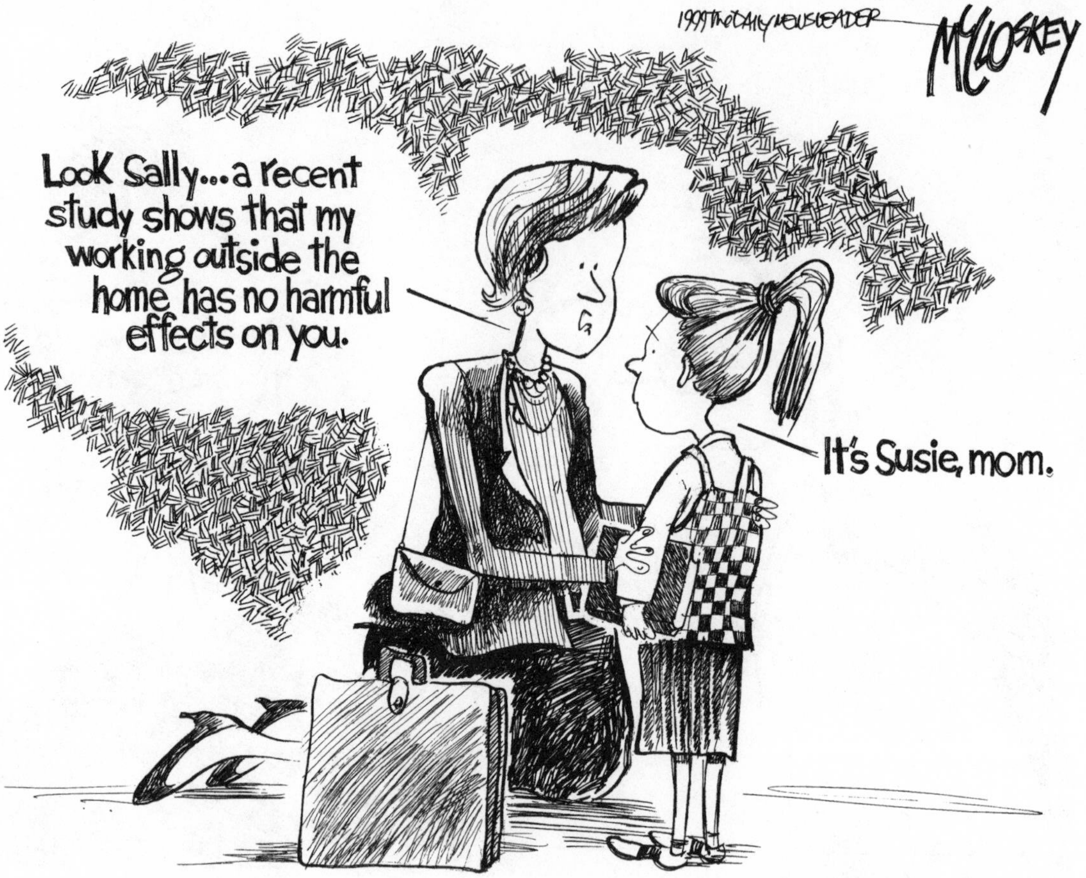

MCCLOSKEY
Look Sally...a recent study shows that my working outside the home has no harmful effects on you.
It's Susie, mom.

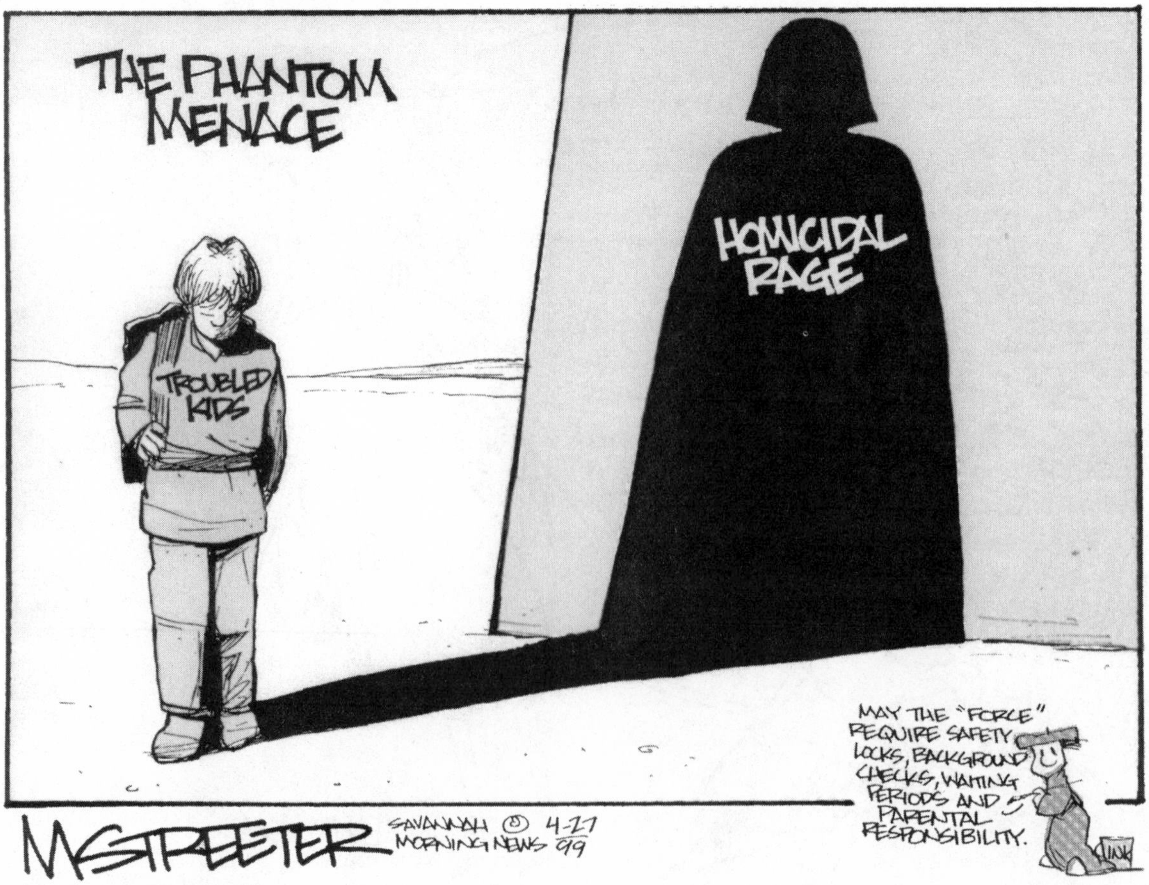

THE PHANTOM MENACE
HOMICIDAL RAGE
TROUBLED KIDS
MAY THE "FORCE" REQUIRE SAFETY LOCKS, BACKGROUND CHECKS, WAITING PERIODS AND PARENTAL RESPONSIBILITY.
INK
MSTREETER
SAVANNAH MORNING NEWS 4-21 '99

MARK STREETER
Courtesy Savannah Morning News

CHESTER COMMODORE
Courtesy Chicago Daily Defender

JIM BORGMAN
Courtesy Cincinnati Enquirer

BRUCE QUAST
Courtesy Rockford Register-Star

PAM WINTERS
Courtesy San Diego Union

122

Crime

Three years ago, the strangled body of six-year-old JonBenet Ramsey was discovered in her parents' expensive home in Boulder, Colorado. In late 1999, a grand jury completed a 13-month investigation into the child's death. The grand jury filed no charges. Its conclusion: There simply was not enough evidence to convict anyone. Parents John and Patsy Ramsey remained suspects, although they maintained their innocence. Boulder police officers, widely criticized for having bungled the early investigation, continued to work on the case.

A Michigan judge sentenced Dr. Jack Kevorkian to 10 to 25 years in prison following his conviction for second-degree murder in a euthanasia case. In contrast to previous incidents in which the so-called Dr. Death merely assisted patients in committing suicide, Kevorkian was convicted of having personally injected the deceased with a lethal drug.

Police treatment of minorities became an issue once again in 1999. Following devastating testimony from fellow officers, a white policeman admitted to having beaten and tortured a Haitian immigrant in New York City. Four white officers were charged in the shooting death of Amador Diallo, an unarmed African immigrant who was struck by 19 bullets in a confrontation with police.

DAVE GRANLUND©1999 METROWEST DAILY NEWS.

DAVE GRANLUND
Courtesy Metrowest Daily News

Still going...

PATRICK RICE
Courtesy Jupiter Courier

CLAY BENNETT
Courtesy Christian Science Monitor

JERRY BARNETT
Courtesy Indianapolis News

HANK McCLURE
Courtesy Lawton Constitution (Okla.)

JIMMY MARGULIES
Courtesy Hackensack Record

125

DAVID REDDICK
Courtesy Anderson Herald Bulletin (Ind.)

DAVID HITCH
Courtesy Worcester Telegram & Gazette (Mass.)

126

Gun Control

Serious crimes that were reported to police dropped by 10 percent in the first half of 1999. According to the FBI, this extended to seven and a half years the continuous decline in crimes nationwide. There appeared to be many reasons for the drop, including more state and local anti-crime measures, a decline in markets for cocaine, and a steadily growing economy.

Controversy continued during the year over the issue of gun control. Congress debated a wide variety of bills dealing with the transfer of ownership of handguns, fitting handguns with child safety locks, banning semiautomatic assault weapons, and allowing tax credits for the purchase of safe storage devices for firearms.

Just as with term limits and campaign financing, however, no meaningful legislation was passed. Both the House and the Senate did approve weak bills calling for a minimum waiting period for firearms sold at gun shows. The House version would require a 24-hour wait while the Senate bill would increase it to 72 hours.

WALT HANDELSMAN
Courtesy New Orleans Times-Picayune

JERRY BARNETT
Courtesy Indianapolis News

JOHN WEISS
Courtesy Scotts Valley Banner

GARY VARVEL
Courtesy Indianapolis Star

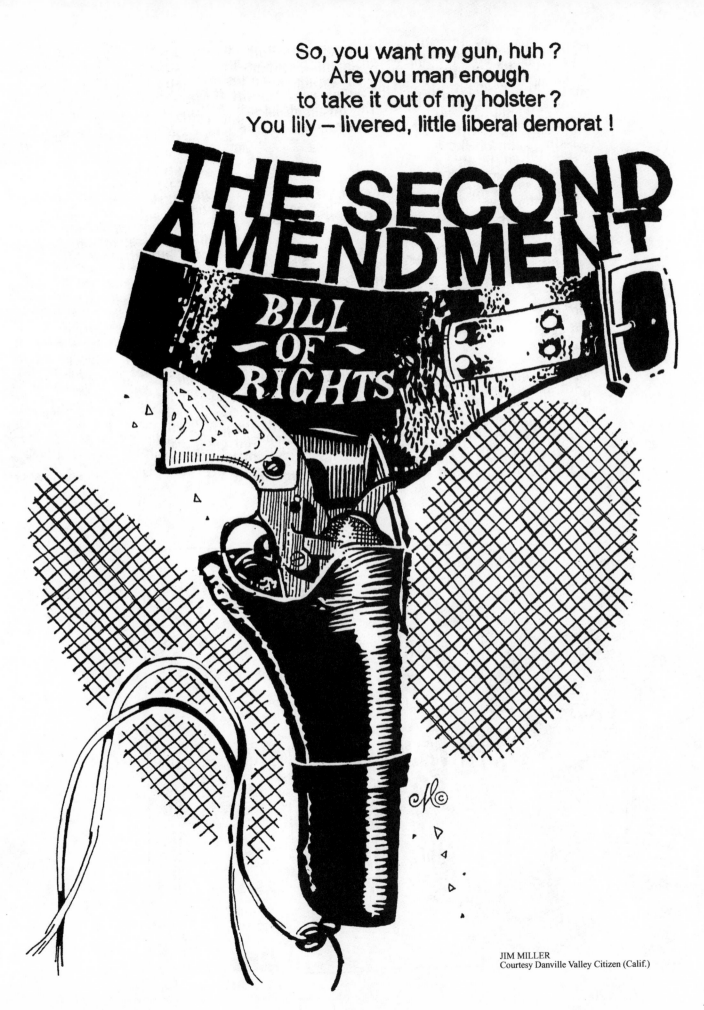

So, you want my gun, huh ?
Are you man enough
to take it out of my holster ?
You lily – livered, little liberal demorat !

JIM MILLER
Courtesy Danville Valley Citizen (Calif.)

YET ANOTHER TOWN WHERE THEY SAID, "IT COULDN'T HAPPEN HERE."

DOUG MacGREGOR
Courtesy News-Press at Fort Myers

GORE WANTS ALL HANDGUN OWNERS TO BE LICENSED

MAY I SEE YOUR LICENSE?

WAYNE STAYSKAL
Courtesy Tampa Tribune

JAKE FULLER
Courtesy Gainesville Sun

JEFF PARKER
Courtesy Florida Today

131

STEPHEN TEMPLETON
Courtesy Fayetteville Observer (N.C.)

JERRY BUCKLEY
Courtesy Express Newspapers

CHESTER COMMODORE
Courtesy Chicago Daily Defender

CLAY BENNETT
Courtesy Christian Science Monitor

CHAN LOWE
Courtesy Sun-Sentinel (Fla.)

LIFE, LIBERTY ...AND THE PURSUIT OF HAPPINESS.

JOE HELLER
Courtesy Green Bay Press-Gazette

CHUCK ASAY
Courtesy Colorado Springs Gazette-Telegraph

SIGNE WILKINSON
Courtesy Philadelphia Daily News

WAYNE STAYSKAL
Courtesy Tampa Tribune

...the right of the people to keep and bear grudges,
shall not be infringed.

JIMMY MARGULIES
Courtesy Hackensack Record

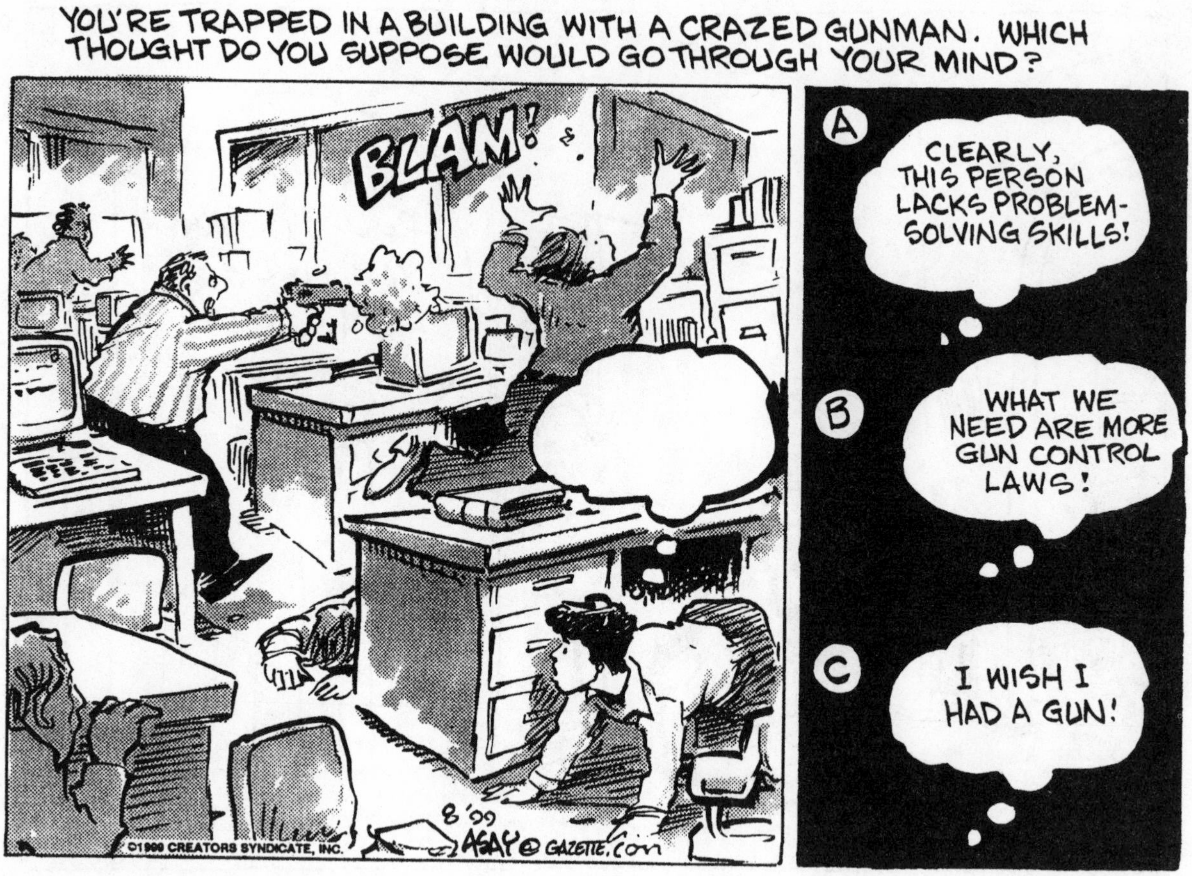
YOU'RE TRAPPED IN A BUILDING WITH A CRAZED GUNMAN. WHICH THOUGHT DO YOU SUPPOSE WOULD GO THROUGH YOUR MIND?
BLAM!
A
CLEARLY, THIS PERSON LACKS PROBLEM-SOLVING SKILLS!
B
WHAT WE NEED ARE MORE GUN CONTROL LAWS!
C
I WISH I HAD A GUN!
©1999 CREATORS SYNDICATE, INC.
8'99
ASAY © GAZETTE.COM

CHUCK ASAY
Courtesy Colorado Springs Gazette-Telegraph

SVEN VAN ASSCHE
Courtesy Darien Times

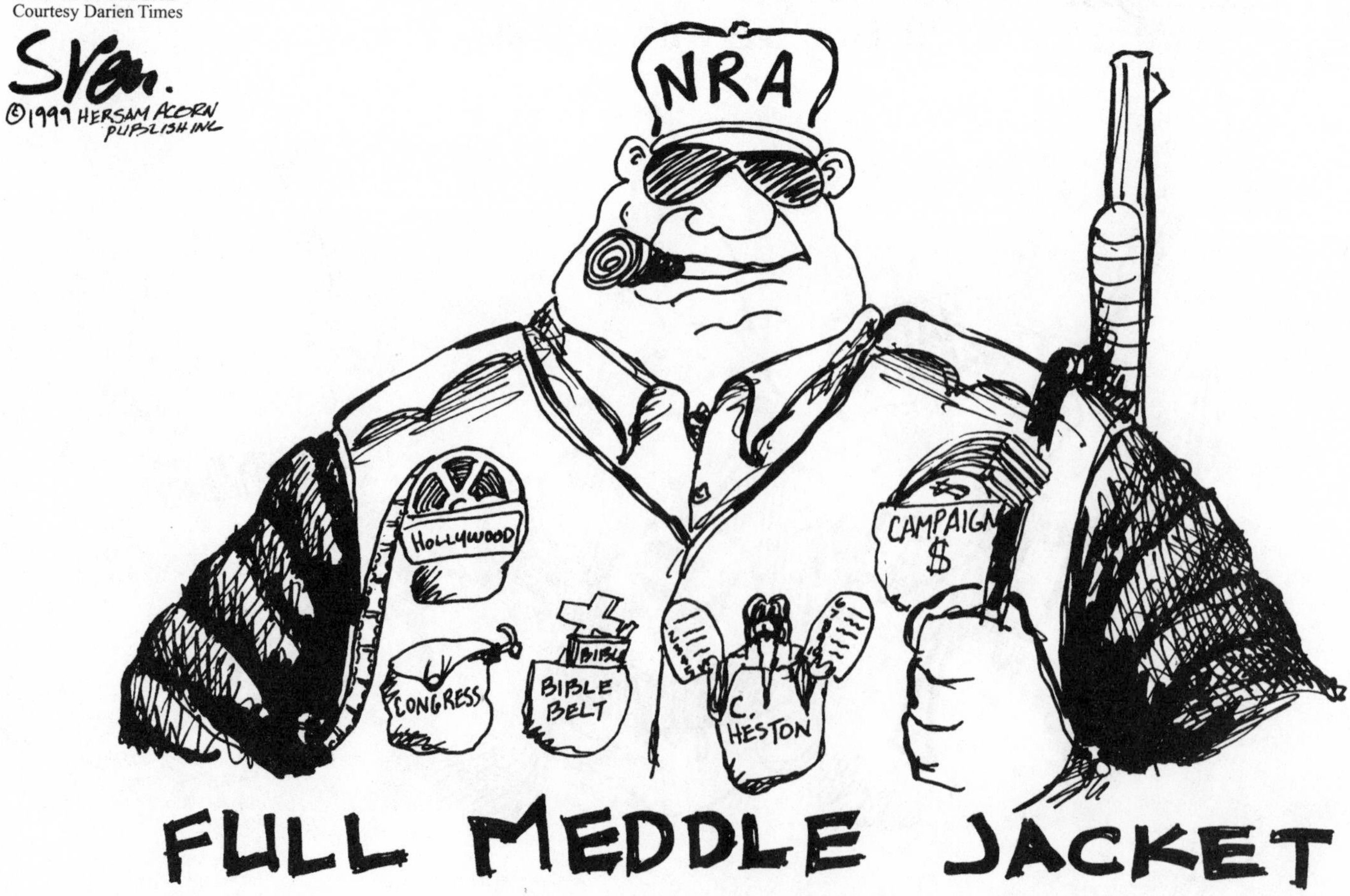
Sven.
©1999 HERSAM ACORN PUBLISHING INC
NRA
HOLLYWOOD
CAMPAIGN $
BIBLE
CONGRESS
BIBLE BELT
C. HESTON
FULL MEDDLE JACKET

JACK HIGGINS
Courtesy Chicago Sun-Times

MIKE THOMPSON
Courtesy Detroit Free Press

137

BRIAN FAIRRINGTON
Courtesy Scripps Howard News Service

ANNETTE BALESTERI
Courtesy Antioch Ledger-Dispatch (Calif.)

JOHN KOVALIC
Courtesy Shetland Productions

STEVE BREEN
Courtesy Asbury Park Press (N.J.)

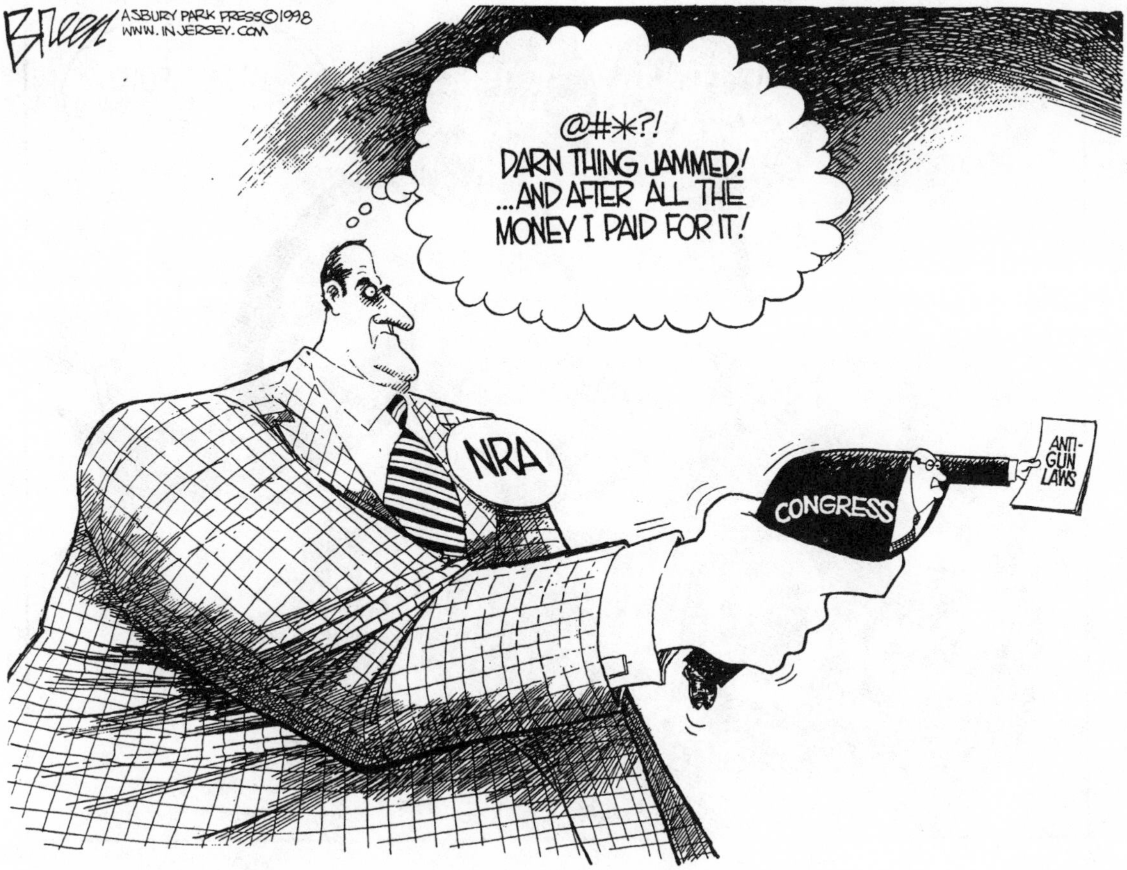
BREEN ASBURY PARK PRESS©1998
WWW.INJERSEY.COM
@#*?!
DARN THING JAMMED!
...AND AFTER ALL THE
MONEY I PAID FOR IT!
NRA
CONGRESS
ANTI-GUN LAWS

MATT DAVIES
Courtesy Journal News (N.Y.)

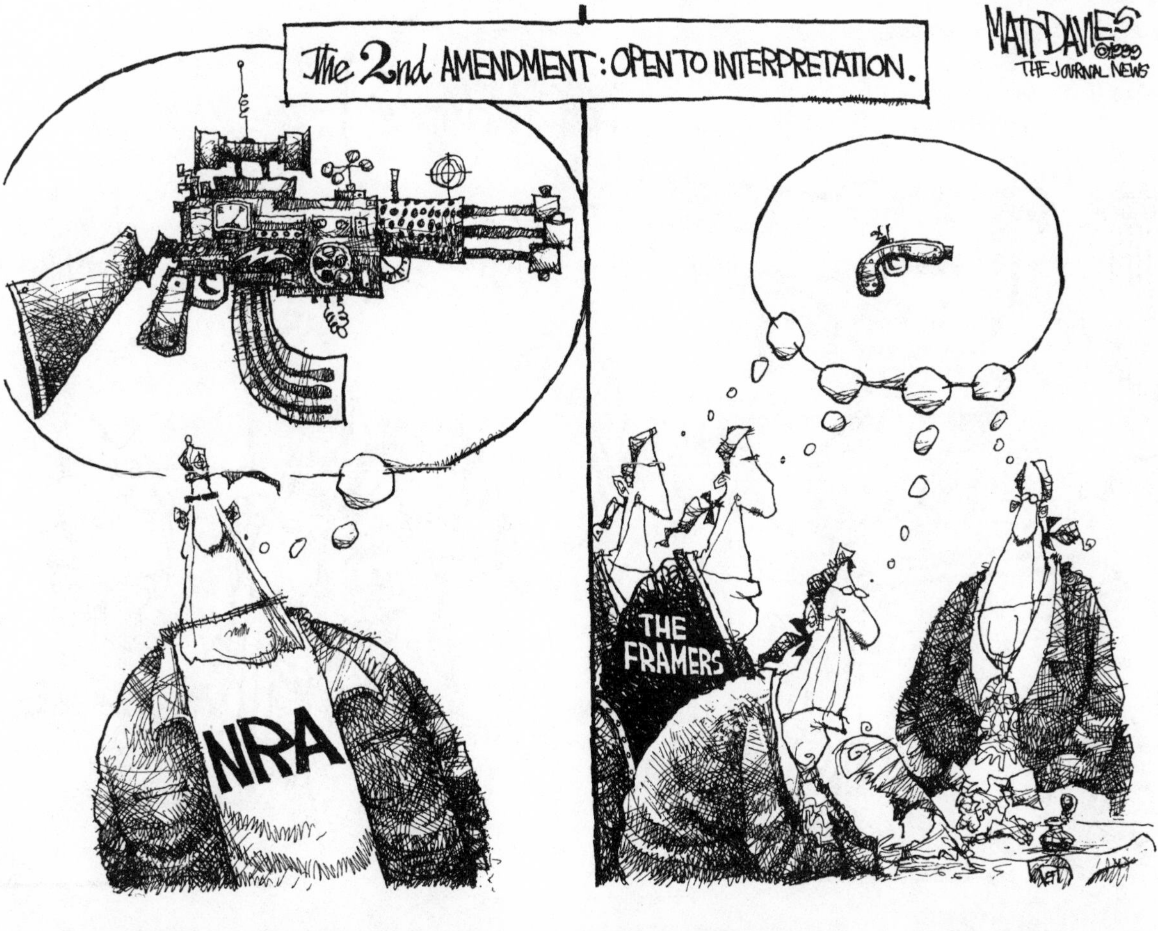
The 2nd AMENDMENT: OPEN TO INTERPRETATION.
MATT DAVIES ©1999 THE JOURNAL NEWS
NRA
THE FRAMERS

DAVID REDDICK
Courtesy Anderson Herald Bulletin (Ind.)

SAM RAWLS
Courtesy Rockdale Citizen (Ga.)

140

The Media

In early November, a Boston television reporter surprised Republican presidential candidate George W. Bush by asking him to name the leaders of Taiwan, India, Chechnya, and Pakistan. The question caught Bush completely off guard, and he was able to name only one—the president of Taiwan. It was a cheap shot, and for many Americans simply confirmed what they already knew—that many interviewers are more interested in promoting their own careers and grabbing headlines than in obtaining information. For some, it has become a game of GOTCHA!

George Stephanopoulas, former communications director in the Clinton White House, agreed that it was a cheap shot and said he doubted that any other candidate could have named all four leaders without prior notice.

A $50 million wrongful death suit was brought against a television show during the year. The show was accused of causing the death of Scott Amedure, who was killed in 1995 after revealing on the program his secret crush on another man.

Surveys show that television sets are on seven hours and twelve minutes a day in the average American household, and that 21 percent of the country's nine-year-olds watch television more than five hours a day. In Europe, the figure is about 11 percent.

MICHAEL RAMIREZ
Courtesy Los Angeles Times

141

BILL WHITEHEAD
Courtesy Kansas City Business Journal

DARYL CAGLE
Courtesy Midweek (Hawaii)

MIKE SMITH
Courtesy Las Vegas Sun

CARLOS E. GARY
Courtesy Daily Herald (Ill.)

KEVIN KALLAUGHER
Courtesy Baltimore Sun

JEFF STAHLER
Courtesy Cincinnati Post

BOB LANG
Courtesy The News-Sentinel (Ind.)

BRUMSIC BRANDON, JR.
Courtesy Florida Today

STEVE BREEN
Courtesy Asbury Park Press (N.J.)

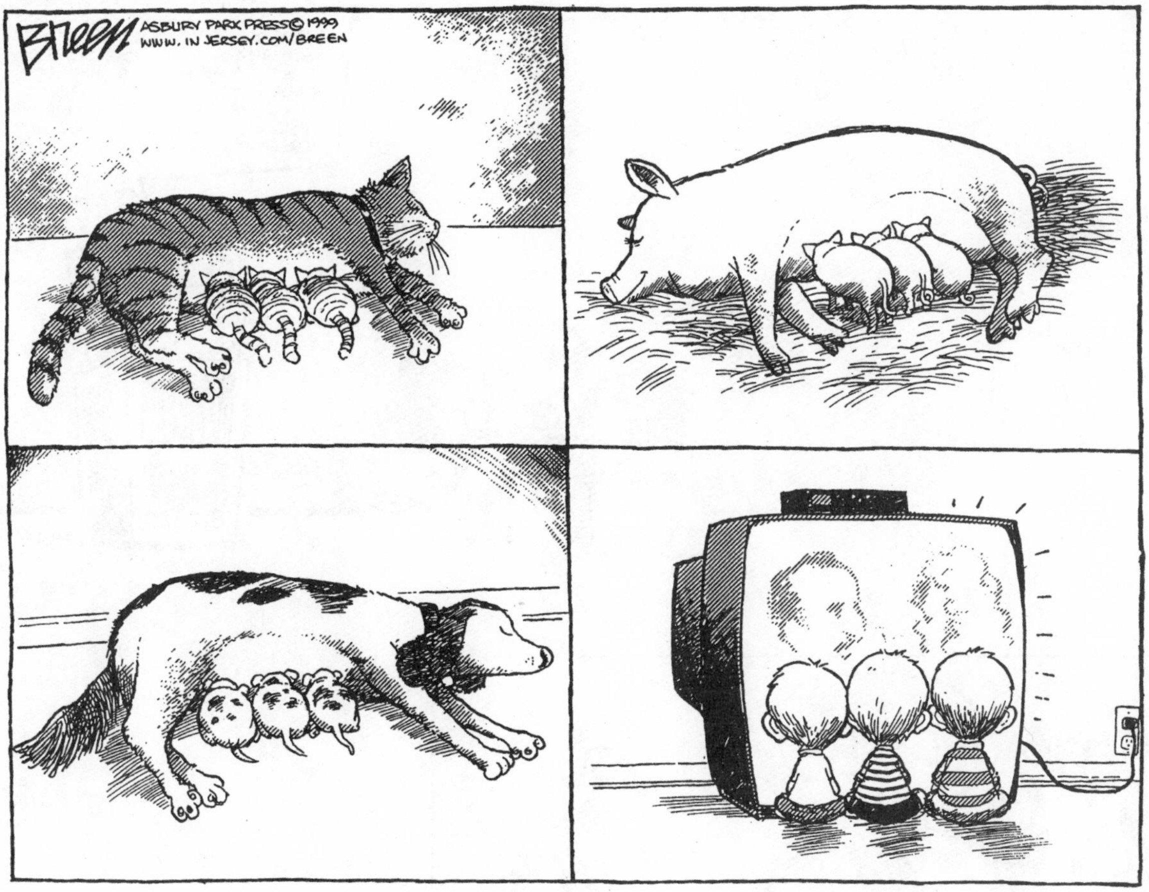
BREEN ASBURY PARK PRESS © 1999 WWW. IN JERSEY.COM/BREEN

JAMES McCLOSKEY
Courtesy Staunton Daily News Leader

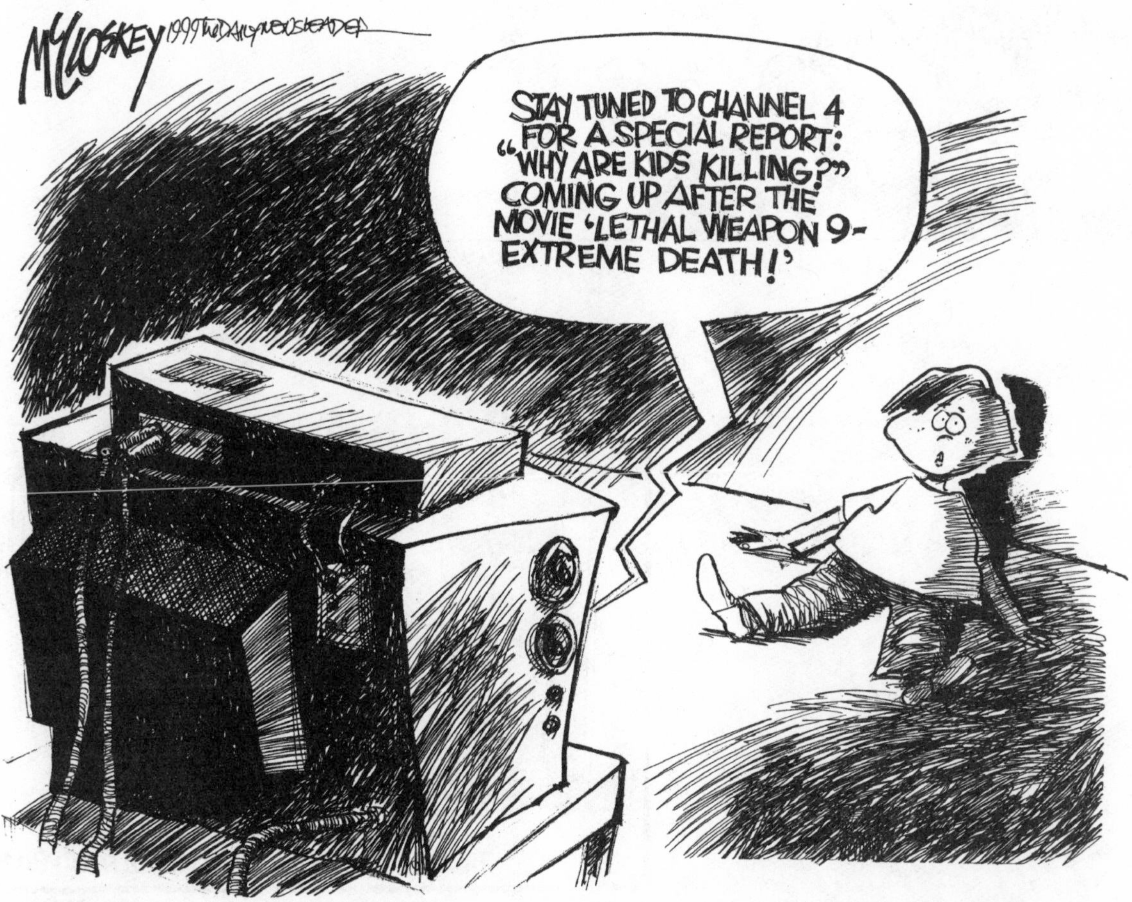
McCLOSKEY 1999 The Daily News Leader
STAY TUNED TO CHANNEL 4 FOR A SPECIAL REPORT: "WHY ARE KIDS KILLING?" COMING UP AFTER THE MOVIE 'LETHAL WEAPON 9- EXTREME DEATH!'

SCOTT BATEMAN
Courtesy North American Syndicate

BRIAN FAIRRINGTON
Courtesy Scripps Howard News Service

BOB ENGLEHART
Courtesy Hartford Courant

JEFF DANZIGER
Courtesy Los Angeles Times Syndicate

ROB ROGERS
Courtesy Pittsburgh Post-Gazette

SAM RAWLS
Courtesy Rockdale Citizen (Ga.)

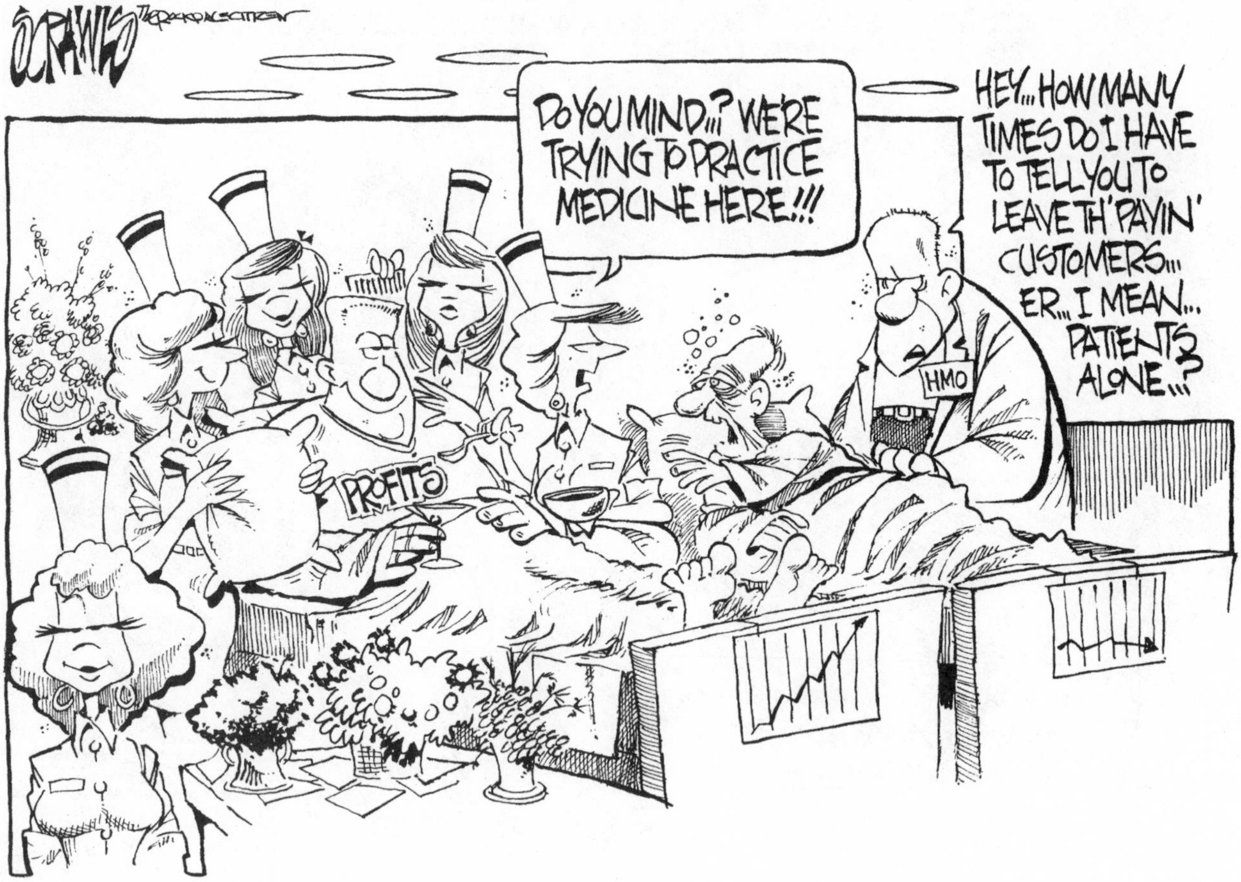
RAWLS
DO YOU MIND...? WE'RE TRYING TO PRACTICE MEDICINE HERE!!!
HEY... HOW MANY TIMES DO I HAVE TO TELL YOU TO LEAVE TH' PAYIN' CUSTOMERS... ER... I MEAN... PATIENTS ALONE...?
PROFITS
HMO

WALT HANDELSMAN
Courtesy New Orleans Times-Picayune

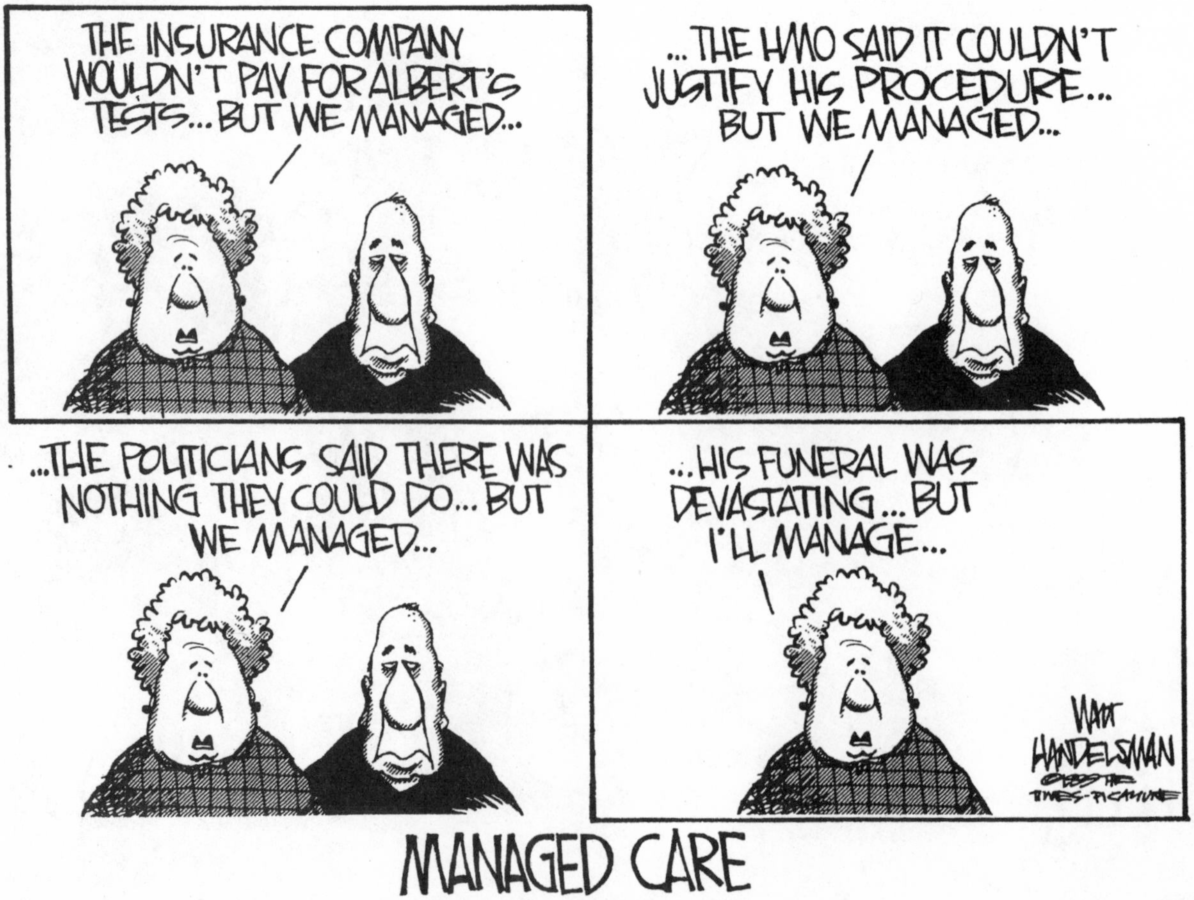
THE INSURANCE COMPANY WOULDN'T PAY FOR ALBERT'S TESTS... BUT WE MANAGED...
...THE HMO SAID IT COULDN'T JUSTIFY HIS PROCEDURE... BUT WE MANAGED...
...THE POLITICIANS SAID THERE WAS NOTHING THEY COULD DO... BUT WE MANAGED...
...HIS FUNERAL WAS DEVASTATING... BUT I'LL MANAGE...
WALT HANDELSMAN
MANAGED CARE

Health

Big Tobacco has agreed to pay $206 billion in settlement money for claims against the tobacco industry, and in late 1999 the way was cleared for participating states to begin collecting.

As a result of incresed competition and the federal government's tightening grip on Medicare reimbursements, HMOs began hiking their rates by about 7 percent across the country. Many of the largest HMOs are now allowing doctors and patients more input into decision-making, rather than giving administrators sole authority. The trend is for insurers to stick to their business and medical providers to stick to theirs.

At the top of the nation's list of health care problems is concern for the 44 million Americans who have no health insurance. They can be found not only among the poor, but in virtually all areas of society. For example, some well educated and healthy young people just beginning their careers assign health insurance low priority. Many feel they don't need it just yet. Congress and the president have taken notice of this and are expected to focus on the problem in the year 2000.

WAYNE STAYSKAL
Courtesy Tampa Tribune

JAMES MERCADO
Courtesy Honolulu Star-Bulletin

WILLIAM L. FLINT
Courtesy Arlington Morning News

ED FISCHER
Courtesy Agri-News

STEVE GREENBERG
Courtesy San Francisco Examiner

DANA SUMMERS
Courtesy Orlando Sentinel

SAM RAWLS
Courtesy Rockdale Citizen (Ga.)

JIM DYKE
Courtesy News Tribune (Mo.)

Education

School shootings continued to rock the nation in 1999. In April, two students at Columbine High School in Littleton, Colorado, members of a so-called group of "outcasts" on campus, walked into the cafeteria and began shooting and throwing pipe bombs. Sixteen people were killed and more than 20 were wounded. A month later, a student in Conyers, Georgia, shot six classmates. Congress moved to tighten gun laws as a mystified society searched for reasons for the violence.

In Kansas, the board of education voted to ban from the classroom all references to evolution. The action resurrected memories of the famous John Scopes "monkey trial" in Tennessee in 1925. Scopes was convicted of teaching evolution but eventually was vindicated by the Supreme Court in 1968.

Early in 1999, the Fifth U.S. Circuit Court of Appeals, which has jurisdiction in Texas, Louisiana, and Mississippi, ruled that students cannot use the school public address system to lead prayers at public events. The edict set off a furor at many schools. When to pray, and when not to pray, in public schools remains a knotty problem because of conflicting court decisions.

ED STEIN
Courtesy Rocky Mountain News

NICK ANDERSON
Courtesy Louisville Courier-Journal

JIM DYKE
Courtesy News Tribune (Mo.)

DANA SUMMERS
Courtesy Orlando Sentinel

CHESTER COMMODORE
Courtesy Chicago Daily Defender

ED STEIN
Courtesy Rocky Mountain News

CINDY PROCIOUS
Courtesy Huntsville Times (Ala.)

MIKE PETERS
Courtesy Dayton Daily News

ALAN VITELLO
Courtesy Greeley Tribune (Colo.)

RICHARD CROWSON
Courtesy Wichita Eagle

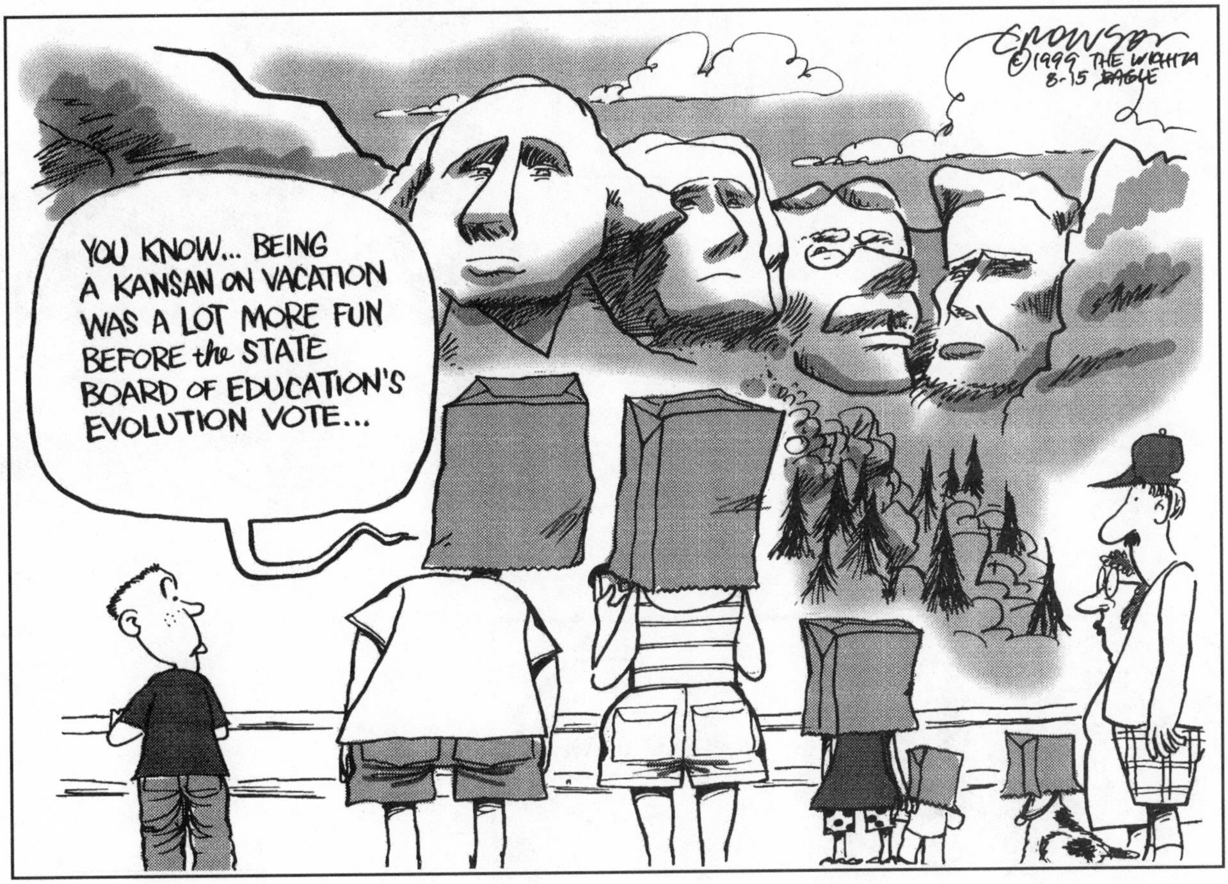
CROWSON ©1999 THE WICHITA EAGLE 8-15
YOU KNOW... BEING A KANSAN ON VACATION WAS A LOT MORE FUN BEFORE the STATE BOARD OF EDUCATION'S EVOLUTION VOTE...

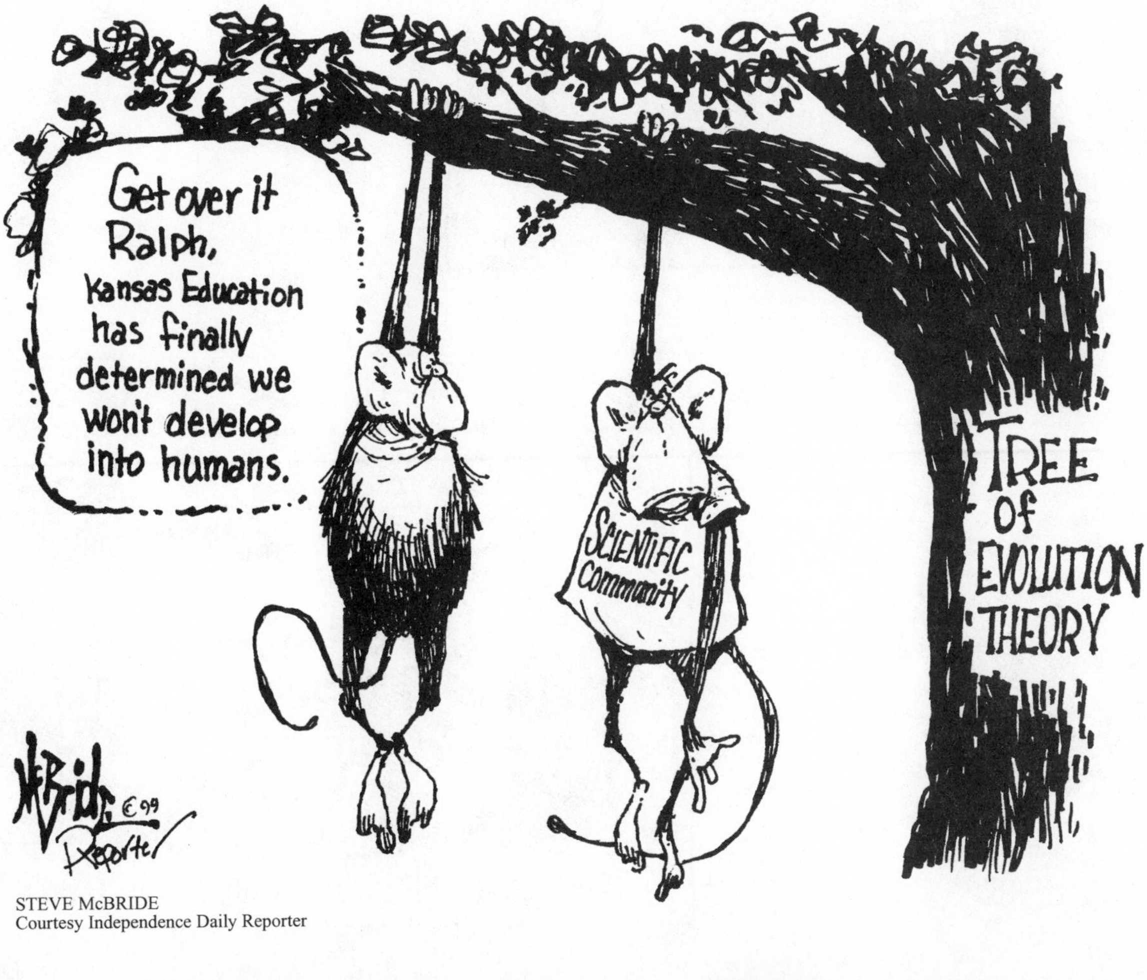
Get over it Ralph, Kansas Education has finally determined we won't develop into humans.
SCIENTIFIC Community
TREE of EVOLUTION THEORY
McBride ©99 Reporter

STEVE McBRIDE
Courtesy Independence Daily Reporter

MARSHALL RAMSEY
Courtesy Jackson Clarion-Ledger (Miss.)

WAYNE STROOT
Courtesy Topeka Capital-Journal

STACY CURTIS
Courtesy The Times (Ind.)

MIKE LUCKOVICH
Courtesy Atlanta Constitution

DAVID CATROW
Courtesy Springfield News (Oh.)

"STUDENTS, PLEASE TAKE OUT YOUR PAPER, MARKERS AND ELEPHANT DUNG—IT'S TIME FOR ART."

DAVID HORSEY
Courtesy Seattle Post-Intelligencer

GLENN McCOY
Courtesy Belleville News-Democrat

MIKE PETERS
Courtesy Dayton Daily News

JEFF KOTERBA
Courtesy Omaha World-Herald

BOB ENGLEHART
Courtesy Hartford Courant

WAYNE STAYSKAL
Courtesy Tampa Tribune

MIKE LUCKOVICH
Courtesy Atlanta Constitution

Sports

The powerful and prestigious International Olympic Committee came under fire for accepting lavish perks, freebies, trips, meals, and gifts from representatives of Salt Lake City in its bid to be selected as host city for the 2002 Winter Olympics. Critics claim this sort of thing has been going on for a long time. The IOC eventually purged 10 members alleged to have received much of the $1.2 million the city spent on "inducements."

The U.S. women's soccer team defeated the Chinese to win the world championship, and the New York Yankees captured the World Series by beating the Atlanta Braves. The Chicago Cubs had one of their worst seasons ever, losing 95 games while winning only 67. The last time the Cubs made it to the World Series was 1945, when they lost to Detroit.

Major league umpires mailed letters of resignation in September in an attempt to force team owners to negotiate a new contract. Officials called their bluff, declined to negotiate, and refused to rescind the resignations of 22 umpires. They, and union leader Richie Phillips, had clearly made a bad call.

Three all-time sports greats—basketball's Michael Jordan, hockey's Wayne Gretzky, and football's John Elway—announced their retirement in 1999.

MIKE THOMPSON
Courtesy Detroit Free Press

PAYNE STEWART 1957-1999

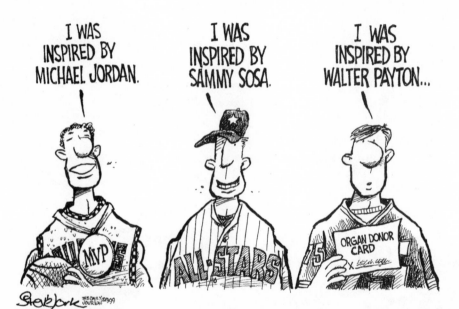

I WAS INSPIRED BY MICHAEL JORDAN.

I WAS INSPIRED BY SAMMY SOSA.

I WAS INSPIRED BY WALTER PAYTON...

ARE YOU ALSO ANNOYED BY CORPORATE IMAGES ADVERTISED ON OUR UNIFORMS?

DICK LOCHER
Courtesy Chicago Tribune

MICHAEL RAMIREZ
Courtesy Los Angeles Times

TOM BECK
Courtesy Freeport Journal-Standard (Ill.)

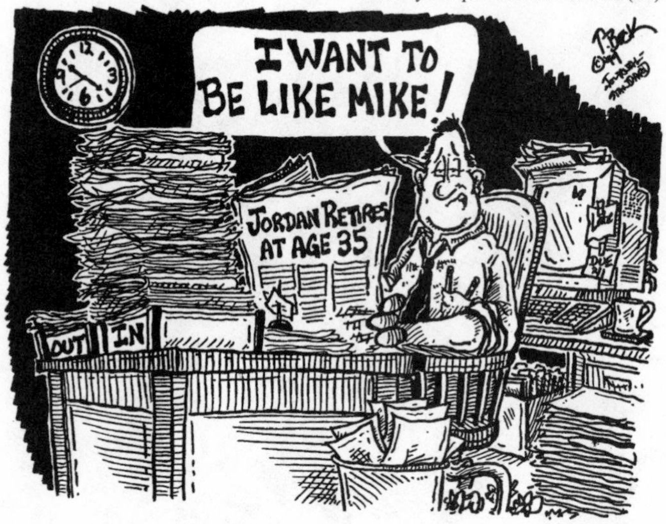
I WANT TO BE LIKE MIKE!
JORDAN RETIRES AT AGE 35
OUT
IN

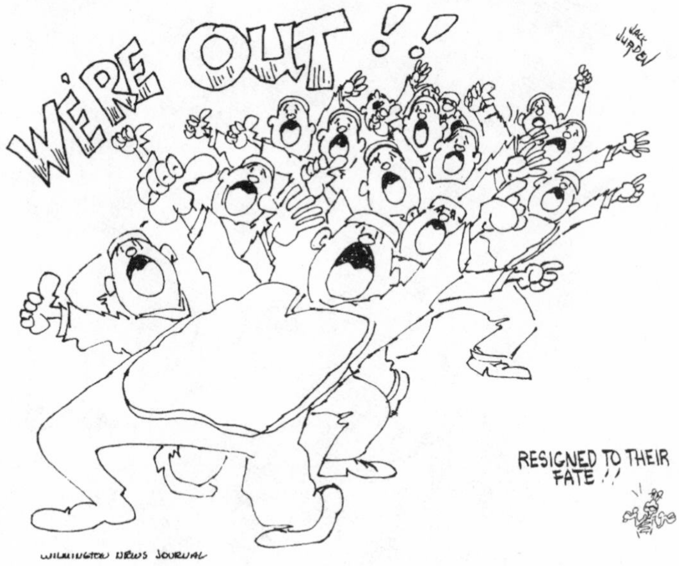
WE'RE OUT!!!
RESIGNED TO THEIR FATE!!
WILMINGTON NEWS JOURNAL

JACK JURDEN
Courtesy Wilmington News Journal

CHIP BOK
Courtesy Akron Beacon Journal

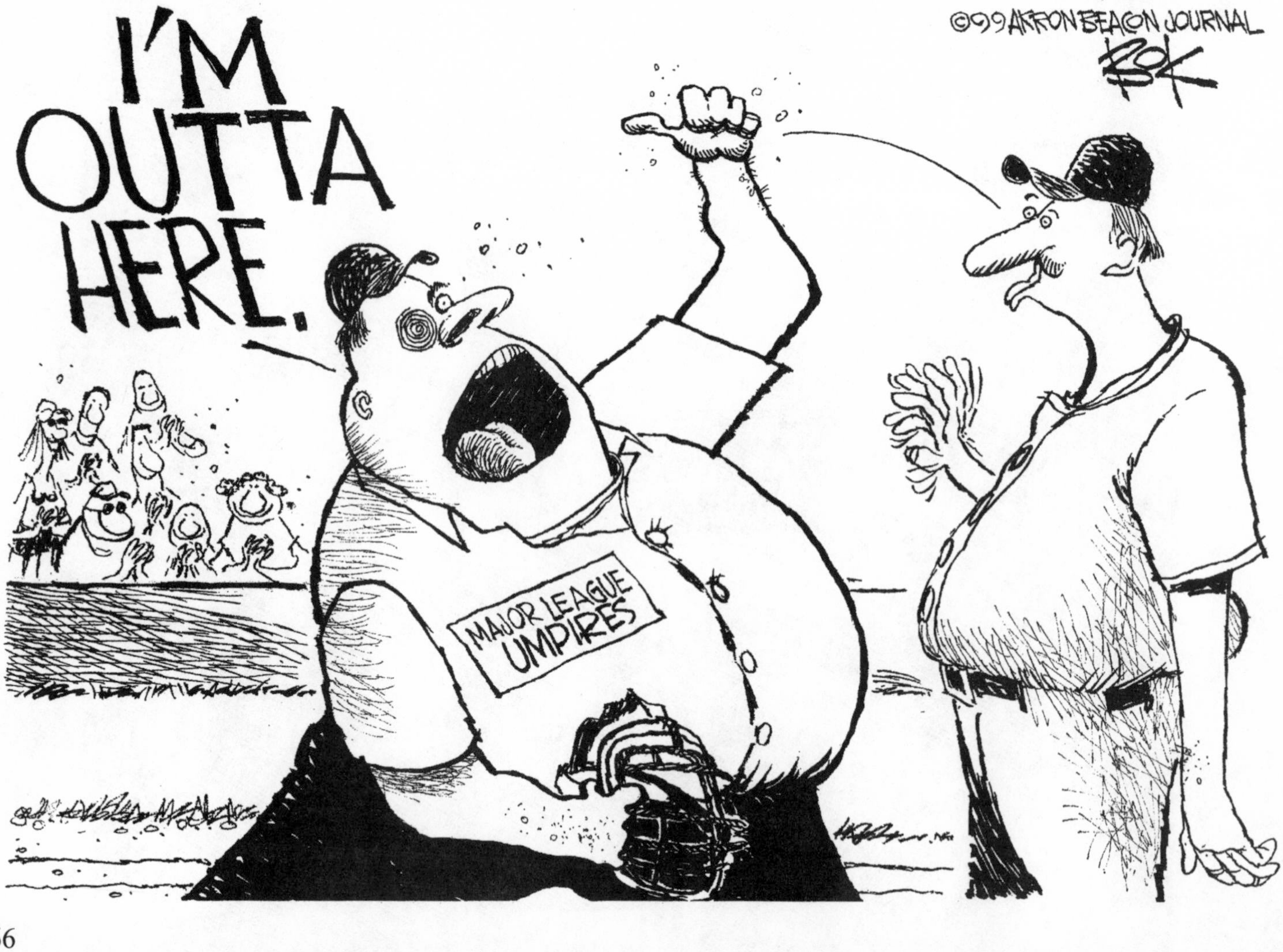
©99 AKRON BEACON JOURNAL
BOK
I'M OUTTA HERE.
MAJOR LEAGUE UMPIRES

STEVEN LAIT
Courtesy Oakland Tribune

SCOTT STANTIS
Courtesy Birmingham News

CLAY JONES
Courtesy Free Lance-Star (Va.)

BRIAN DUFFY
Courtesy Des Moines Register

This **OLYMPIC** bribery thing is a real Scandal!...
As a potential participating athlete I'm shocked that these officials would do something that jeopardizes the integrity of the Games!

DON MARQUIS
Courtesy Paradise Post (Calif.)

Space and Air Travel

NASA suffered a major setback when, after a nine-month voyage of 416 million miles, the $125 million Mars Climate Orbiter vanished after skimming the upper Martian atmosphere. A navigation error, apparently the result of using the wrong system of measurement, sent the probe too close to Mars. American astronauts left water, computers, clothes, and other supplies on the international space station for its first live-in crew's arrival in 2000.

Russia's space program found itself virtually bankrupt, and Eileen Collins became the first woman to command a NASA shuttle mission. Some airlines, responding to complaints from passengers allergic to peanuts, stopped passing out the nuts on flights.

Seven American Airlines mechanics were charged with helping to smuggle cocaine and heroin into the U.S. from Colombia. Twelve past and current Delta Air Lines workers were charged with smuggling cocaine through Puerto Rico.

Airline studies have shown that frequent flyers often are frequent wine drinkers, so some companies have begun to offer passengers a variety of wines, including chardonnay and even French champagne.

DICK LOCHER
Courtesy Chicago Tribune

CLAY JONES
Courtesy Free Lance-Star (Va.)

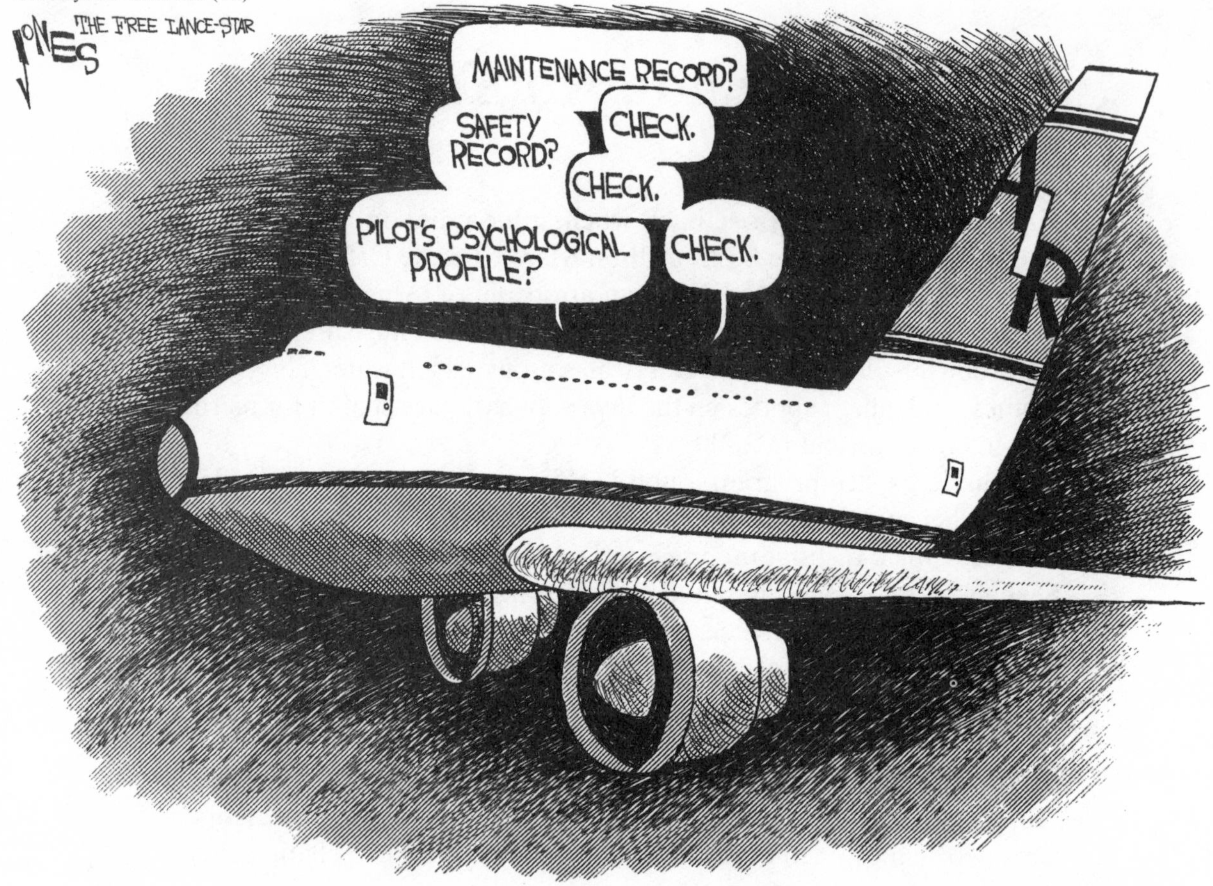
JONES THE FREE LANCE-STAR
MAINTENANCE RECORD?
CHECK.
SAFETY RECORD?
CHECK.
PILOT'S PSYCHOLOGICAL PROFILE?
CHECK.
AIR

ROB CHAMBERS
Courtesy The Signal (Calif.)

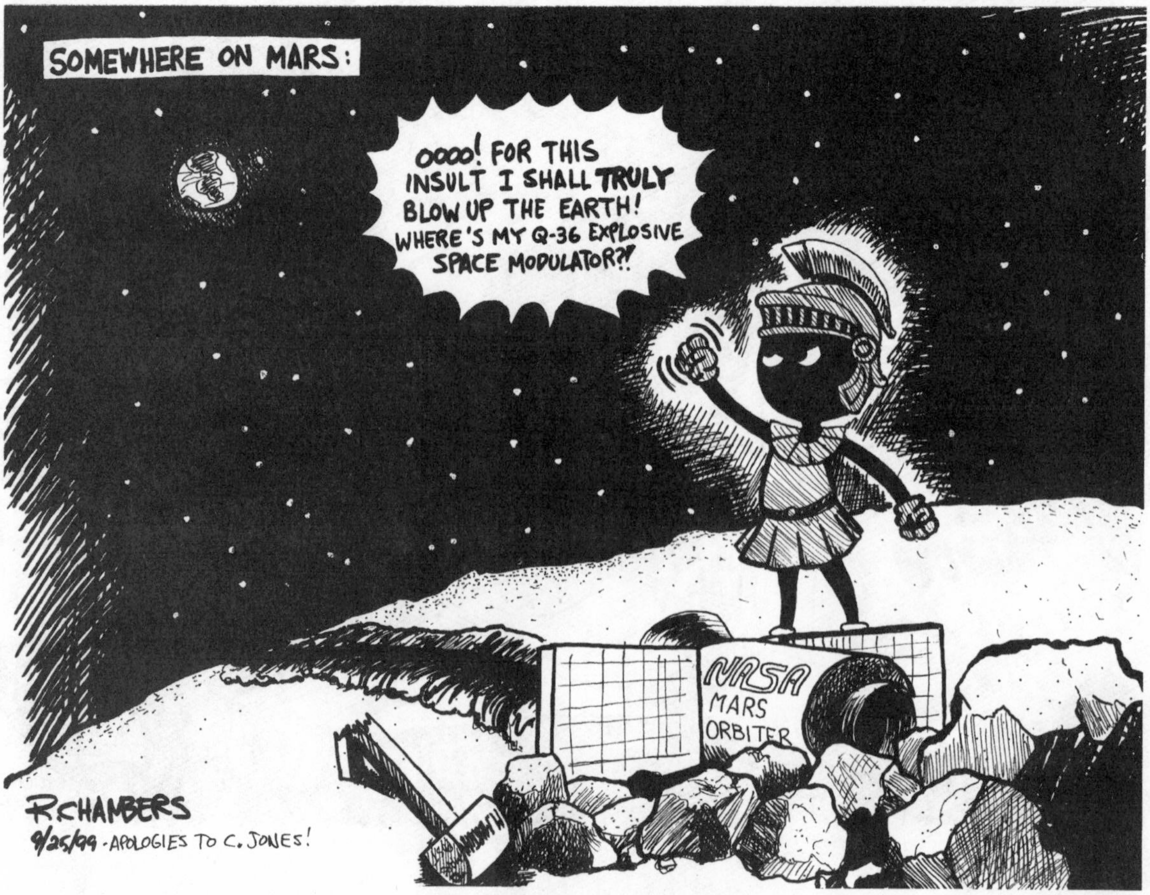
SOMEWHERE ON MARS:
OOOO! FOR THIS INSULT I SHALL TRULY BLOW UP THE EARTH! WHERE'S MY Q-36 EXPLOSIVE SPACE MODULATOR?!
NASA
MARS ORBITER
R. CHAMBERS
9/25/99 - APOLOGIES TO C. JONES!

BOB ENGLEHART
Courtesy Hartford Courant

JACK JURDEN
Courtesy Wilmington News Journal

LINDA BOILEAU
Courtesy Frankfort State Journal

FRED CURATOLO
Courtesy Edmonton Sun (Alberta)

JOE HELLER
Courtesy Green Bay Press-Gazette

172

TOM GIBB
Courtesy Johnstown Tribune-Democrat

ANALYSTS EXAMINE EQUIPMENT CONNECTED WITH THE FAILED MARS ORBITER AND THE JAPANESE URANIUM PLANT ACCIDENT AND REMOVE THE FAULTY PART........

RICK McKEE
Courtesy Augusta Chronicle

"IT NEVER FAILS: I GO UP IN SPACE FOR A FEW DAYS AND HAVE TO COME HOME TO A SINKFUL OF DIRTY DISHES...."

JIM BERTRAM
Courtesy St. Cloud Times (Minn.)

JEFF STAHLER
Courtesy Cincinnati Post

JOHN SPENCER
Courtesy Philadelphia Business Journal

The Military

Peacekeeping forays by the United Nations continued to expand during the year. And since the United States has to furnish most of the equipment and much of the personnel, U.S. forces are being spread all over—in Somalia, Rwanda, Bosnia, Kosovo, Haiti, Iraq, Korea, and now East Timor. Once the troops are in, there seems to be no way to withdraw them.

Because of large cutbacks in military spending by President Clinton, America's armed forces lack the manpower and equipment to serve as global policeman. When U.S. planes bombed civilian targets by mistake, it turned out that the CIA had been using outdated maps to plan the strikes.

After six months of investigation by a congressional panel headed by Rep. Christopher Cox, a classified report concluded that China had been stealing U.S. high-tech military secrets for years, and continues to do so. Clearly, Congress and other government agencies have been lax in protecting the nation's secrets and in allowing businesses to give them away.

The Chinese efforts have focused on obtaining top-of-the-line computers, fiber optics, and advanced electronics-switching technology in addition to missile-guidance systems.

It was disclosed that Lt. Kendra Williams apparently became the first female to launch a missile in combat in the opening salvo of Operation Desert Fox.

STEVE McBRIDE
Courtesy Independence Daily Reporter

ROB ROGERS
Courtesy Pittsburgh Post-Gazette

JOHN SHERFFIUS
Courtesy St. Louis Post-Dispatch

TIM HARTMAN
Courtesy North Hills News Record (Pa.)

JEFF MALLETT
Courtesy Booth News Service

JON RICHARDS
Courtesy Santa Fe Reporter

JIM LANGE
Courtesy Daily Oklahoman

CHIP BOK
Courtesy Akron Beacon Journal

178

RANDY BISH
Courtesy Tribune-Review (Pa.)

ETTA HULME
Courtesy Fort Worth Star-Telegram

TARGET PRACTICE AT THE CIA

KIRK ANDERSON
Courtesy St. Paul Pioneer Press

179

W. A. HOGAN
Courtesy Daily Gleaner (New Bruns.)

STEVE NEASE
Courtesy Windsor Star

Canada

Canada accepts 225,000 legal immigrants each year, a number larger in proportion to its population that any other Western country. Several incidents in which large numbers of Chinese were smuggled in, however, gave rise to loud protests. Last year, 23,838 asylum-seekers were brought in by smuggling rings, and the Canadian government has been giving them work permits, welfare, and health insurance if they were granted asylum. A much harder position, however, was adopted in 1999.

In Quebec, a judge struck down a law requiring that French be the predominant language used on signs, and ruled that English and French words could be the same size. A ban by the European Trade Union on products ranging from chocolate to mineral water from Canada and the U.S. was rescinded by the World Trade Organization.

Canada joined in the effort to bring peace to the Balkans by sending troops and equipment to that troubled area. A lady in Ontario made news when she gave birth to octuplets. And Canada's minister of health announced that smoking adversely affects sexual performance. Quebec still has language police who check to make sure that French is spoken, and Canada continues to suffer from brain drain as skilled workers look for better-paying jobs in the U.S.

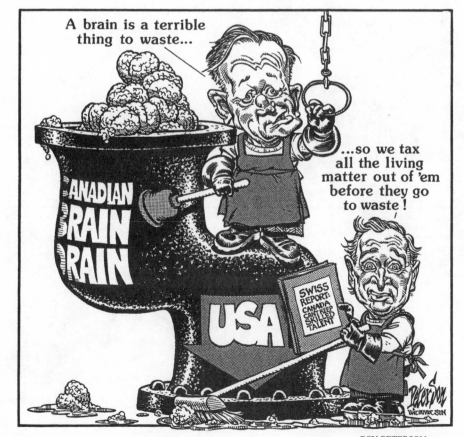

ROY PETERSON
Courtesy Vancouver Sun

STEVE NEASE
Courtesy St. Johns Telegraph-Journal

ANDY DONATO
Courtesy Toronto Sun

W. A. HOGAN
Courtesy Daily Gleaner (New Bruns.)

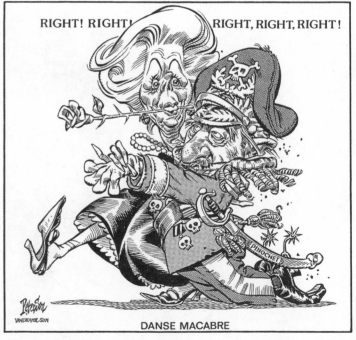

ROY PETERSON
Courtesy Vancouver Sun

STEVE NEASE
Courtesy Montreal Gazette

ANDY DONATO
Courtesy Toronto Sun

DENNY PRITCHARD
Courtesy Brockville Recorder & Times (Ont.)

W. A. HOGAN
Courtesy Daily Gleaner (New Bruns.)

QUEBEC WANTS GOLF TERMS IN FRENCH...

STEVE NEASE
Courtesy Montreal Gazette

W. A. HOGAN
Courtesy National Post (Tor.)

... and Other Issues

Questions associated with Y2K loomed large throughout much of the year. The problem arose from the fact that many computer programs recognized only the last two digits of a year and could read the digits "00" as 1900 instead of 2000. In late November, the U.S. government issued a report declaring that 99 percent of its mission-critical systems were ready for the new year. Only minor problems were reported when the new year dawned.

Edmund Morris published an authorized biography of the fortieth U.S. president entitled *Dutch: A Memoir of Ronald Reagan*. The author inserted a fictionalized version of himself into Reagan's life, frequently blurring the line between fact and fiction. Late in the year, cartoonist Charles Schulz of "Peanuts" fame announced his retirement.

New York Mayor Rudy Giuliani led an assault on the Brooklyn Museum of Art for hosting an exhibit that included a portrait of the Virgin Mary decorated with elephant dung. The mayor threatened to cancel $7 million in museum funding and expel the institution from its city-owned building. First Lady Hillary Clinton, who indicated she would oppose Giuliani in the U.S. Senate race in 2000, sided with the museum.

John F. Kennedy, Jr., died in July in the mysterious crash of a single-engine Piper Saratoga he was piloting. Joe DiMaggio, the Yankee Clipper and one of baseball's all-time greats, passed away after a lengthy illness. Other notables who died in 1999 included Wilt Chamberlain, Walter Payton, George C. Scott, Allen Funt, Al Hirt, Yehudi Menuhin, Stanley Kubrick, Pee Wee Reese, Payne Stewart, and Jordan's King Hussein.

GARY MARKSTEIN
Courtesy Milwaukee Journal Sentinel

CHAN LOWE
Courtesy Sun-Sentinel (Fla.)

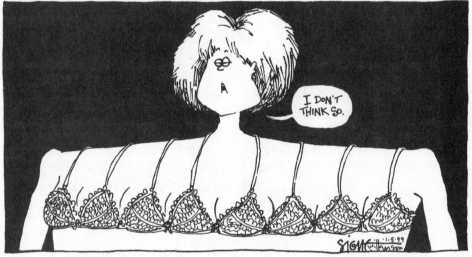

SIGNE WILKINSON
Courtesy Philadelphia Daily News

JERRY HOLBERT
Courtesy Boston Herald

186

RUSSELL HODIN
Courtesy New Times (Calif.)

ROB ROGERS
Courtesy Pittsburgh Post-Gazette

187

RANDY BISH
Courtesy Tribune-Review (Pa.)

STEVE YORK
Courtesy Kankakee Daily Journal

JOE HOFFECKER
Courtesy Cincinnati Business Courier

RANDY BISH
Courtesy Tribune-Review (Pa.)

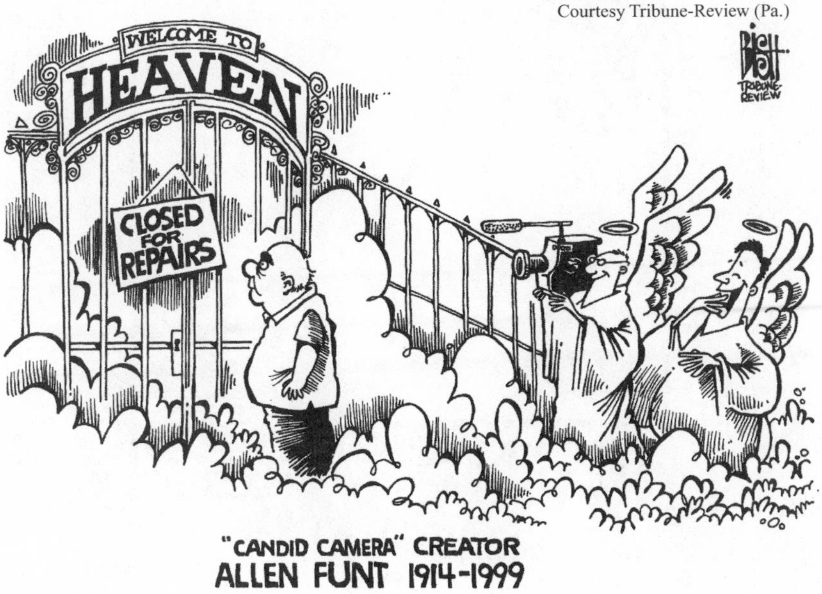
WELCOME TO
HEAVEN
CLOSED FOR REPAIRS
"CANDID CAMERA" CREATOR
ALLEN FUNT 1914-1999

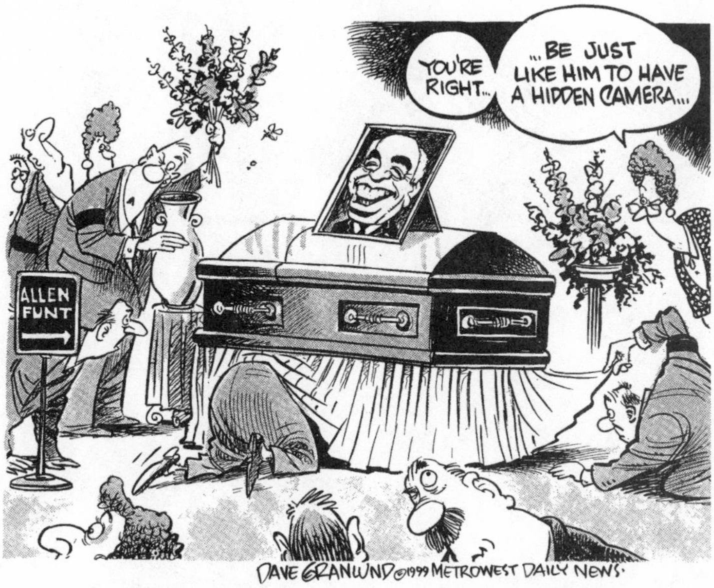
YOU'RE RIGHT...
...BE JUST LIKE HIM TO HAVE A HIDDEN CAMERA...
ALLEN FUNT
DAVE GRANLUND©1999 METROWEST DAILY NEWS

DAVE GRANLUND
Courtesy Metrowest Daily News

WALT HANDELSMAN
Courtesy New Orleans Times-Picayune

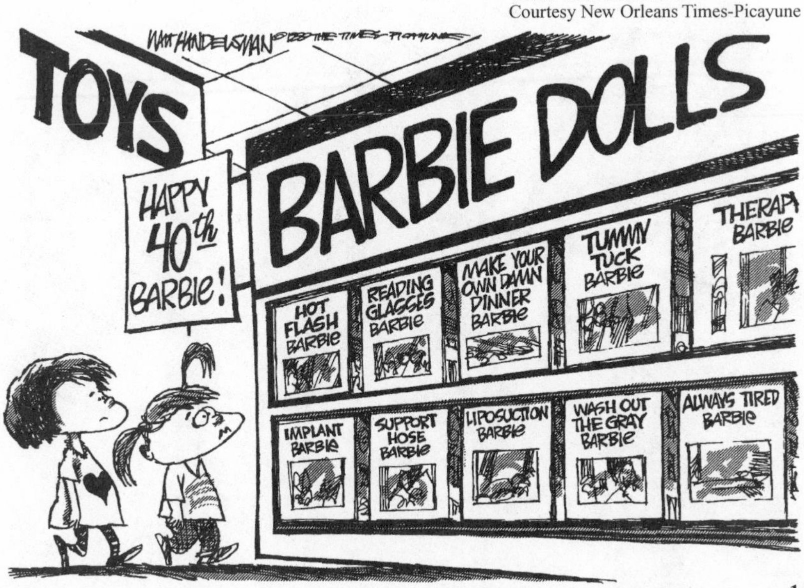
TOYS
BARBIE DOLLS
HAPPY 40th BARBIE!
HOT FLASH BARBIE
READING GLASSES BARBIE
MAKE YOUR OWN DAMN DINNER BARBIE
TUMMY TUCK BARBIE
IMPLANT BARBIE
SUPPORT HOSE BARBIE
LIPOSUCTION BARBIE
WASH OUT THE GRAY BARBIE
ALWAYS TIRED BARBIE

BRIAN DUFFY
Courtesy Des Moines Register

VIC HARVILLE
Courtesy Arkansas Democrat-Gazette

DICK WALLMEYER
Courtesy Long Beach Press-Telegram

BILL GARNER
Courtesy Washington Times

DAVE GRANLUND
Courtesy Metrowest Daily News

JIM BUSH
Courtesy Providence Journal

CHIP BOK
Courtesy Akron Beacon Journal

192

JAMES McCLOSKEY
Courtesy Staunton Daily News Leader

DOUG MacGREGOR
Courtesy News-Press at Fort Myers

Joe DiMaggio
1914 – 1999

J. R. ROSE
Courtesy Byrd Newspapers

WILL O'TOOLE
Courtesy Home News & Tribune (N.J.)

RICK McKEE
Courtesy Augusta Chronicle

JOE DIMAGGIO, 1914-1999

JOHN SHERFFIUS
Courtesy St. Louis Post-Dispatch

RICKY NOBILE
Courtesy Bolivar Commercial (Miss.)

BRIAN FAIRRINGTON
Courtesy Scripps Howard News Service

EUGENE PAYNE
Courtesy Charlotte Observer

ED GAMBLE
Courtesy Florida Times-Union

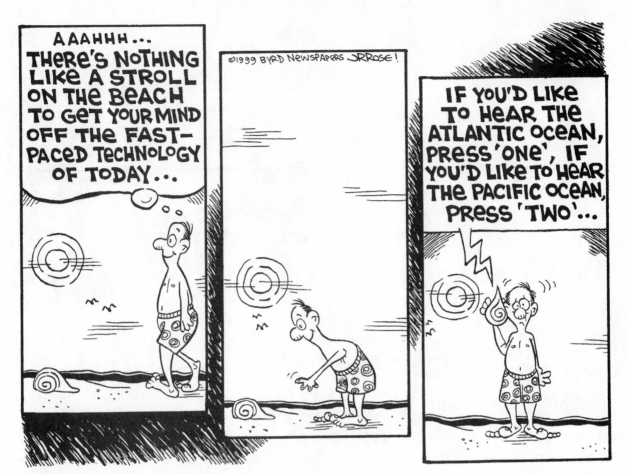

J. R. ROSE
Courtesy Byrd Newspapers

JOHN BRANCH
Courtesy San Antonio Express-News

MIKE RITTER
Courtesy Tribune Newspapers

MIKE THOMPSON
Courtesy Detroit Free Press

TIM HARTMAN
Courtesy North Hills News Record (Pa.)

JOHN SHERFFIUS
Courtesy St. Louis Post-Dispatch

NICK ANDERSON
Courtesy Louisville Courier-Journal

JFK JR'S PLANE IS MISSING...

DICK WALLMEYER
Courtesy Long Beach Press-Telegram

JIM BORGMAN
Courtesy Cincinnati Enquirer

REST IN PEACE, JOHN-JOHN

JOE MAJESKI
Courtesy Wilkes-Barre Times Leader

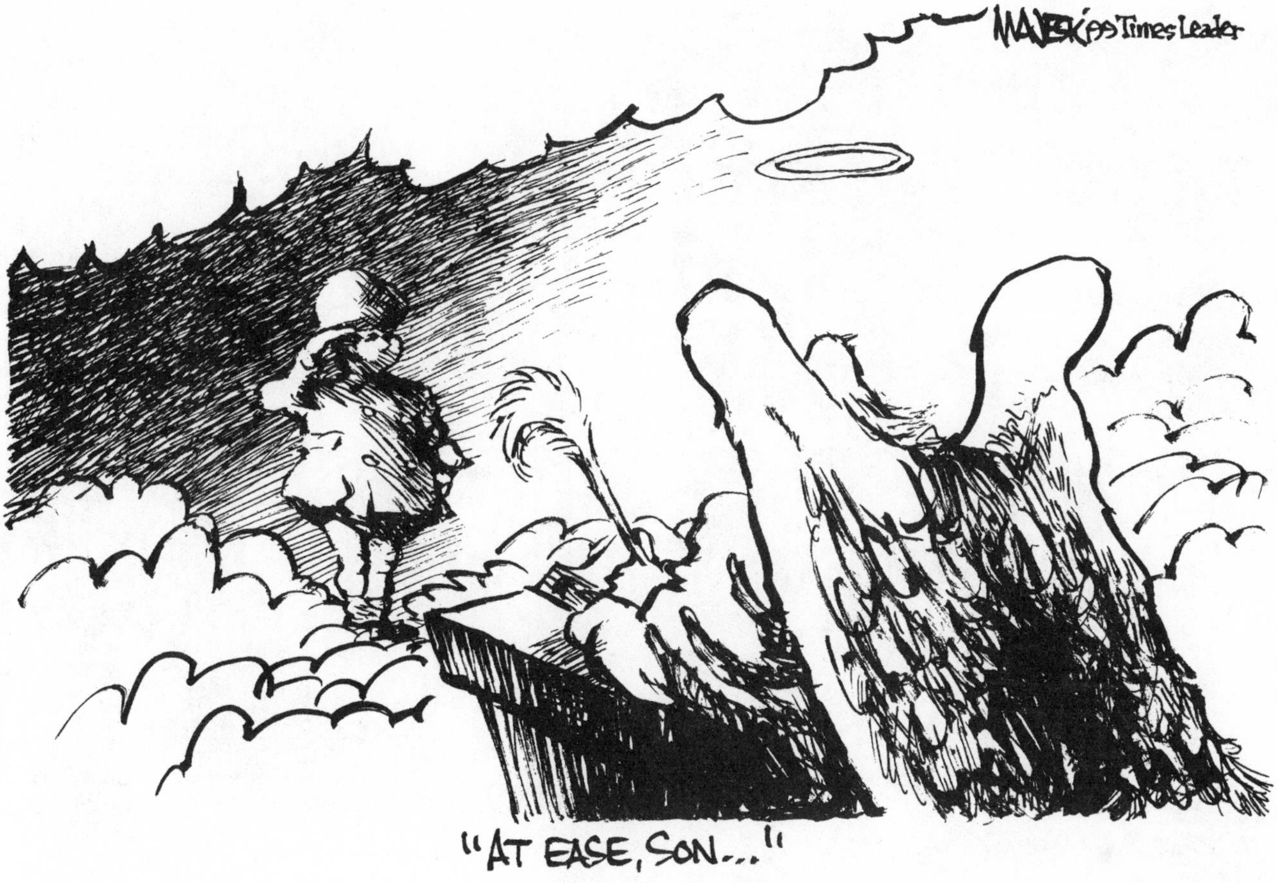
MAJESKI 99 Times Leader
"AT EASE, SON..."

DICK LOCHER
Courtesy Chicago Tribune

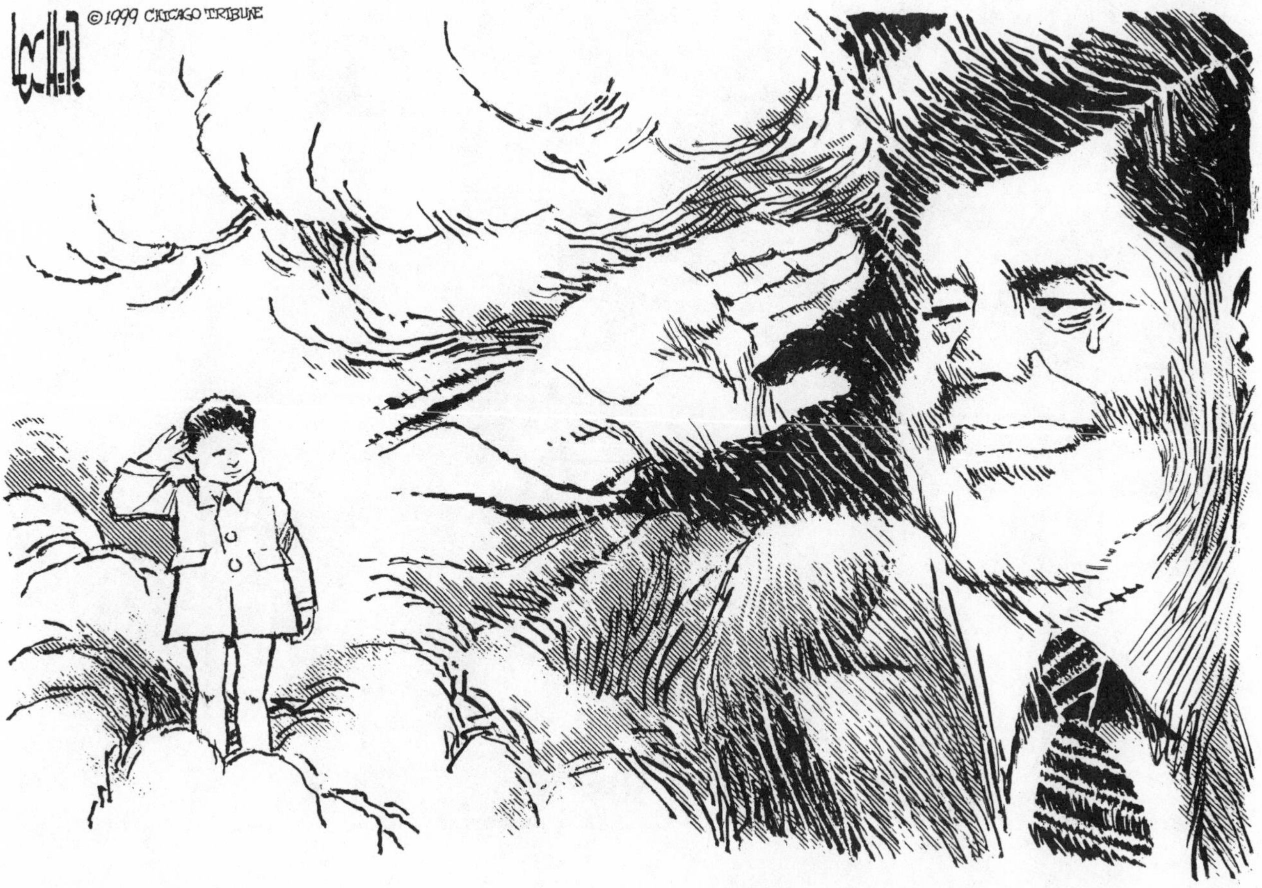
LOCHER ©1999 CHICAGO TRIBUNE

PAUL CONRAD
Courtesy Los Angeles Times Syndicate

JOHN KNUDSEN
Courtesy St. Louis Review

JOHN, WE HARDLY KNEW YE.

LIFE
IS SHORT
ETERNITY
IS FOREVER

MESSAGE FROM CAMELOT

JOHNNY...
WE HARDLY
KNEW YE.

© 1999 CHICAGO SUN-TIMES HIGGINS

JACK HIGGINS
Courtesy Chicago Sun-Times

Past Award Winners

PULITZER PRIZE

1922—Rollin Kirby, New York World
1923—No award given
1924—J.N. Darling, New York Herald-Tribune
1925—Rollin Kirby, New York World
1926—D.R. Fitzpatrick, St. Louis Post-Dispatch
1927—Nelson Harding, Brooklyn Eagle
1928—Nelson Harding, Brooklyn Eagle
1929—Rollin Kirby, New York World
1930—Charles Macauley, Brooklyn Eagle
1931—Edmund Duffy, Baltimore Sun
1932—John T. McCutcheon, Chicago Tribune
1933—H.M. Talburt, Washington Daily News
1934—Edmund Duffy, Baltimore Sun
1935—Ross A. Lewis, Milwaukee Journal
1936—No award given
1937—C.D. Batchelor, New York Daily News
1938—Vaughn Shoemaker, Chicago Daily News
1939—Charles G. Werner, Daily Oklahoman
1940—Edmund Duffy, Baltimore Sun
1941—Jacob Burck, Chicago Times
1942—Herbert L. Block, NEA
1943—Jay N. Darling, New York Herald-Tribune
1944—Clifford K. Berryman, Washington Star
1945—Bill Mauldin, United Features Syndicate
1946—Bruce Russell, Los Angeles Times
1947—Vaughn Shoemaker, Chicago Daily News
1948—Reuben L. ("Rube") Goldberg, New York Sun
1949—Lute Pease, Newark Evening News
1950—James T. Berryman, Washington Star
1951—Reginald W. Manning, Arizona Republic
1952—Fred L. Packer, New York Mirror
1953—Edward D. Kuekes, Cleveland Plain Dealer
1954—Herbert L. Block, Washington Post
1955—Daniel R. Fitzpatrick, St. Louis Post-Dispatch
1956—Robert York, Louisville Times
1957—Tom Little, Nashville Tennessean
1958—Bruce M. Shanks, Buffalo Evening News
1959—Bill Mauldin, St. Louis Post-Dispatch
1960—No award given
1961—Carey Orr, Chicago Tribune
1962—Edmund S. Valtman, Hartford Times
1963—Frank Miller, Des Moines Register
1964—Paul Conrad, Denver Post
1965—No award given
1966—Don Wright, Miami News
1967—Patrick B. Oliphant, Denver Post
1968—Eugene Gray Payne, Charlotte Observer
1969—John Fischetti, Chicago Daily News
1970—Thomas F. Darcy, Newsday
1971—Paul Conrad, Los Angeles Times
1972—Jeffrey K. MacNelly, Richmond News Leader
1973—No award given
1974—Paul Szep, Boston Globe
1975—Garry Trudeau, Universal Press Syndicate
1976—Tony Auth, Philadelphia Enquirer
1977—Paul Szep, Boston Globe

1978—Jeff MacNelly, Richmond News Leader
1979—Herbert Block, Washington Post
1980—Don Wright, Miami News
1981—Mike Peters, Dayton Daily News
1982—Ben Sargent, Austin American-Statesman
1983—Dick Locher, Chicago Tribune
1984—Paul Conrad, Los Angeles Times
1985—Jeff MacNelly, Chicago Tribune
1986—Jules Feiffer, Universal Press Syndicate
1987—Berke Breathed, Washington Post Writers Group
1988—Doug Marlette, Atlanta Constitution
1989—Jack Higgins, Chicago Sun-Times
1990—Tom Toles, Buffalo News
1991—Jim Borgman, Cincinnati Enquirer
1992—Signe Wilkinson, Philadelphia Daily News
1993—Steve Benson, Arizona Republic
1994—Michael Ramirez, Memphis Commercial Appeal
1995—Mike Luckovich, Atlanta Constitution
1996—Jim Morin, Miami Herald
1997—Walt Handelsman, New Orleans Times-Picayune
1998—Steve Breen, Asbury Park Press
1999—David Horsey, Seattle Post-Intelligencer

NATIONAL SOCIETY OF PROFESSIONAL JOURNALISTS AWARD (SIGMA DELTA CHI AWARD)

1942—Jacob Burck, Chicago Times
1943—Charles Werner, Chicago Sun
1944—Henry Barrow, Associated Press
1945—Reuben L. Goldberg, New York Sun
1946—Dorman H. Smith, NEA
1947—Bruce Russell, Los Angeles Times
1948—Herbert Block, Washington Post
1949—Herbert Block, Washington Post
1950—Bruce Russell, Los Angeles Times
1951—Herbert Block, Washington Post and
      Bruce Russell, Los Angeles Times
1952—Cecil Jensen, Chicago Daily News
1953—John Fischetti, NEA
1954—Calvin Alley, Memphis Commercial Appeal
1955—John Fischetti, NEA
1956—Herbert Block, Washington Post
1957—Scott Long, Minneapolis Tribune
1958—Clifford H. Baldowski, Atlanta Constitution
1959—Charles G. Brooks, Birmingham News
1960—Dan Dowling, New York Herald-Tribune
1961—Frank Interlandi, Des Moines Register
1962—Paul Conrad, Denver Post
1963—William Mauldin, Chicago Sun-Times
1964—Charles Bissell, Nashville Tennessean
1965—Roy Justus, Minneapolis Star
1966—Patrick Oliphant, Denver Post
1967—Eugene Payne, Charlotte Observer

1968—Paul Conrad, Los Angeles Times
1969—William Mauldin, Chicago Sun-Times
1970—Paul Conrad, Los Angeles Times
1971—Hugh Haynie, Louisville Courier-Journal
1972—William Mauldin, Chicago Sun-Times
1973—Paul Szep, Boston Globe
1974—Mike Peters, Dayton Daily News
1975—Tony Auth, Philadelphia Enquirer
1976—Paul Szep, Boston Globe
1977—Don Wright, Miami News
1978—Jim Borgman, Cincinnati Enquirer
1979—John P.Trever, Albuquerque Journal
1980—Paul Conrad, Los Angeles Times
1981—Paul Conrad, Los Angeles Times
1982—Dick Locher, Chicago Tribune
1983—Rob Lawlor, Philadelphia Daily News
1984—Mike Lane, Baltimore Evening Sun
1985—Doug Marlette, Charlotte Observer
1986—Mike Keefe, Denver Post
1987—Paul Conrad, Los Angeles Times
1988—Jack Higgins, Chicago Sun-Times
1989—Don Wright, Palm Beach Post
1990—Jeff MacNelly, Chicago Tribune
1991—Walt Handelsman, New Orleans Times-Picayune
1992—Robert Ariail, Columbia State
1993—Herbert Block, Washington Post
1994—Jim Borgman, Cincinnati Enquirer
1995—Michael Ramirez, Memphis Commercial Appeal
1996—Paul Conrad, Los Angeles Times
1997—Michael Ramirez, Los Angeles Times
1998—Jack Higgins, Chicago Sun-Times

FISCHETTI AWARD

1982—Lee Judge, Kansas City Times
1983—Bill DeOre, Dallas Morning News
1984—Tom Toles, Buffalo News
1985—Scott Willis, Dallas Times-Herald
1986—Doug Marlette, Charlotte Observer
1987—Dick Locher, Chicago Tribune
1988—Arthur Bok, Akron Beacon-Journal
1989—Lambert Der, Greenville News
1990—Jeff Stahler, Cincinnati Post
1991—Mike Keefe, Denver Post
1992—Doug Marlette, New York Newsday
1993—Bill Schorr, Kansas City Star
1994—John Deering, Arkansas Democrat-Gazette
1995—Stuart Carlson, Milwaukee Journal Sentinel
1996—Jimmy Margulies, The Record, New Jersey
1997—Gary Markstein, Milwaukee Journal Sentinel
1998—Jack Higgins, Chicago Sun-Times
1999—Nick Anderson, Louisville Courier-Journal

NATIONAL NEWSPAPER AWARD/CANADA

1949—Jack Boothe, Toronto Globe and Mail
1950—James G. Reidford, Montreal Star
1951—Len Norris, Vancouver Sun
1952—Robert La Palme, Le Devoir, Montreal
1953—Robert W. Chambers, Halifax Chronicle-Herald
1954—John Collins, Montreal Gazette
1955—Merle R. Tingley, London Free Press
1956—James G. Reidford, Toronto Globe and Mail
1957—James G. Reidford, Toronto Globe and Mail
1958—Raoul Hunter, Le Soleil, Quebec
1959—Duncan Macpherson, Toronto Star
1960—Duncan Macpherson, Toronto Star
1961—Ed McNally, Montreal Star
1962—Duncan Macpherson, Toronto Star
1963—Jan Kamienski, Winnipeg Tribune
1964—Ed McNally, Montreal Star
1965—Duncan Macpherson, Toronto Star
1966—Robert W. Chambers, Halifax Chronicle-Herald
1967—Raoul Hunter, Le Soleil, Quebec
1968—Roy Peterson, Vancouver Sun
1969—Edward Uluschak, Edmonton Journal
1970—Duncan Macpherson, Toronto Daily Star
1971—Yardley Jones, Toronto Daily Star
1972—Duncan Macpherson, Toronto Star
1973—John Collins, Montreal Gazette
1974—Blaine, Hamilton Spectator
1975—Roy Peterson, Vancouver Sun
1976—Andy Donato, Toronto Sun
1977—Terry Mosher, Montreal Gazette
1978—Terry Mosher, Montreal Gazette
1979—Edd Uluschak, Edmonton Journal
1980—Vic Roschkov, Toronto Star
1981—Tom Innes, Calgary Herald
1982—Blaine, Hamilton Spectator
1983—Dale Cummings, Winnipeg Free Press
1984—Roy Peterson, Vancouver Sun
1985—Ed Franklin, Toronto Globe and Mail
1986—Brian Gable, Regina Leader-Post
1987—Raffi Anderian, Ottawa Citizen
1988—Vance Rodewalt, Calgary Herald
1989—Cameron Cardow, Regina Leader-Post
1990—Roy Peterson, Vancouver Sun
1991—Guy Badeaux, Le Droit, Ottawa
1992—Bruce Mackinnon, Halifax Herald
1993—Bruce Mackinnon, Halifax Herald
1994—Roy Peterson, Vancouver Sun
1995—Brian Gable, Toronto Globe and Mail
1996—Roy Peterson, Vancouver Sun
1997—Serge Chapleau, La Presse
1998—Roy Peterson, Vancouver Sun

Index of Cartoonists

INDEX OF CARTOONISTS

Complete Your CARTOON COLLECTION

Previous editions of this timeless series are available for those wishing to update their collection of the most provocative moments of the past twenty-five years. In the early days the topics were the oil crisis, Richard Nixon's presidency, Watergate, and the Vietnam War. Over time the cartoonists and their subjects have changed right along with the presidential administrations. These days those subjects have been replaced by the Clinton administration, Bosnia, O. J. Simpson, and the environment. But in the end, the wit and wisdom of the editorial cartoonists has prevailed. And on the pages of these op-ed galleries one can find memories and much more from the nation's best cartoonists.

Select from the following supply of past editions

_____ 1972 Edition $16.95 pb (F)	_____ 1983 Edition out of stock	_____ 1993 Edition $14.95 pb
_____ 1974 Edition $16.95 pb (F)	_____ 1984 Edition $16.95 pb (F)	_____ 1994 Edition $14.95 pb
_____ 1975 Edition $16.95 pb (F)	_____ 1985 Edition $16.95 pb (F)	_____ 1995 Edition $14.95 pb
_____ 1976 Edition $16.95 pb (F)	_____ 1986 Edition $16.95 pb (F)	_____ 1996 Edition $14.95 pb
_____ 1977 Edition $16.95 pb (F)	_____ 1987 Edition $14.95 pb	_____ 1997 Edition $14.95 pb
_____ 1978 Edition $16.95 pb (F)	_____ 1988 Edition $14.95 pb	_____ 1998 Edition $14.95 pb
1979 Edition out of stock	_____ 1989 Edition $16.95 pb (F)	_____ 1999 Edition $14.95 pb
_____ 1980 Edition $16.95 pb (F)	_____ 1990 Edition $14.95 pb	_____ Add me to the list of standing orders for future editions.
_____ 1981 Edition $16.95 pb (F)	_____ 1991 Edition $14.95 pb	
_____ 1982 Edition $16.95 pb (F)	_____ 1992 Edition $14.95 pb	

Please include $2.75 for 4th Class Postage and handling or $5.35 for UPS Ground Shipment plus $.75 for each additional copy ordered.

Total enclosed: _____

NAME _____

ADDRESS _____

CITY_____ STATE_____ ZIP_____

Make checks payable to:

PELICAN PUBLISHING COMPANY
P.O. Box 3110, Dept. 6BEC
Gretna, Louisiana 70054-3110

CREDIT CARD ORDERS CALL 1-800-843-1724

Jefferson Parish residents add 8¾% tax. All other Louisiana residents add 4% tax.